H. Casser-Jayne **STILL LIFE**

For Becky, a true vision, and for EZ who saw the vision.
A *special* thanks to Paul V. Chiles
With great appreciation to the re-enactors

Copyright © 2005 hcj studios, inc.
All rights reserved. No part of this
publication may be reproduced or
transmitted in any form or by any
means, electronic or mechanical,
without written permission from
the publisher.

Library of Congress Cataloging-in-Publication Data
Casser-Jayne, Halli
ISBN-0-976-5960-0-8

Design by Le Petit Cochon Productions

All photographs are gelatin-silver prints.

Printed and bound in China.

FIRST EDITION

"A peace above all earthly dignities,
A still and quiet conscience."

- William Shakespeare, Henry VIII

"O lost, and by the wind grieved, ghost,
come back again."

- Thomas Wolfe, Look Homeward Angel

forward

"Although I spend the better part of my days on the land that is known as Antietam National Battlefield, and know the battlefield and its environs as well as anyone, I must admit I was stunned upon viewing the photographs that are this book. They made me, forced me, to look in an unfamiliar way at that which I look at nearly every day. The view is that of an artist's eye, not a historian's perspective. I was awed and excited by the photographs and knew I wanted to be a part of this project. How refreshing a viewpoint. Emotional? Yes. And yet the vision of H. Casser-Jayne is defined, clear, and has even caught the technical and tactical within the confines of the art.

On September 17, 1862, all the horrors of the world fell onto the fields and woods that make up Antietam National Battlefield. War had come to the Valley of the Antietam; fear, honor, sacrifice, and death came to this peaceful land and would change it forever. Soldiers of both the Union and Confederacy marched to this place and in the blink of an eye became a part of history. On paper, armies are made up of regiments and batteries; in realty they are made up of individual men. They are the lonely men who in most cases are far from their homes, far from the ones they love, far from the lives they remember. They wear butternut or blue and march in unending lines to an uncertain fate in the silent hours that precede the battle.

At Sharpsburg, when the silence broke, the concept of war would change forever. Gone was the civility of this Civil War, ahead lay a day of savagery that few had ever conceived possible. Today, as you walk the fields of Antietam and view the waving cornfields or listen to the singing of the birds, it is hard to imagine what happened on this very ground in 1862. But we must not forget. On this hollow land defined only by simple wooden fences was the stage for one of the most devastating 12 hours in American history.

Forget not the faces of the men who fought here; do not allow them to become a long line of blue or gray marching to our memory. We must remember these shoemakers, store clerks and farmers who fought here, these city and country boys who bled into this rich brown earth one hot Septembers' day. These are the men who made this place different from all the rest, they have forever changed it. They are the men of Antietam. God bless them all.

In *Still Life*, you will meet the ghosts of these men, as well as their wives, sisters, brothers, girlfriends. Joshua Chamberlain of the 20th Maine wrote, "That in great events, something abides..." H. Casser-Jayne has captured the spirit that inhabits the battlefield landscape. What is portrayed stands as a new monument to those who fought and to those who help us remember.

John Howard, Superintendent Antietam and Monocacy Battlefields

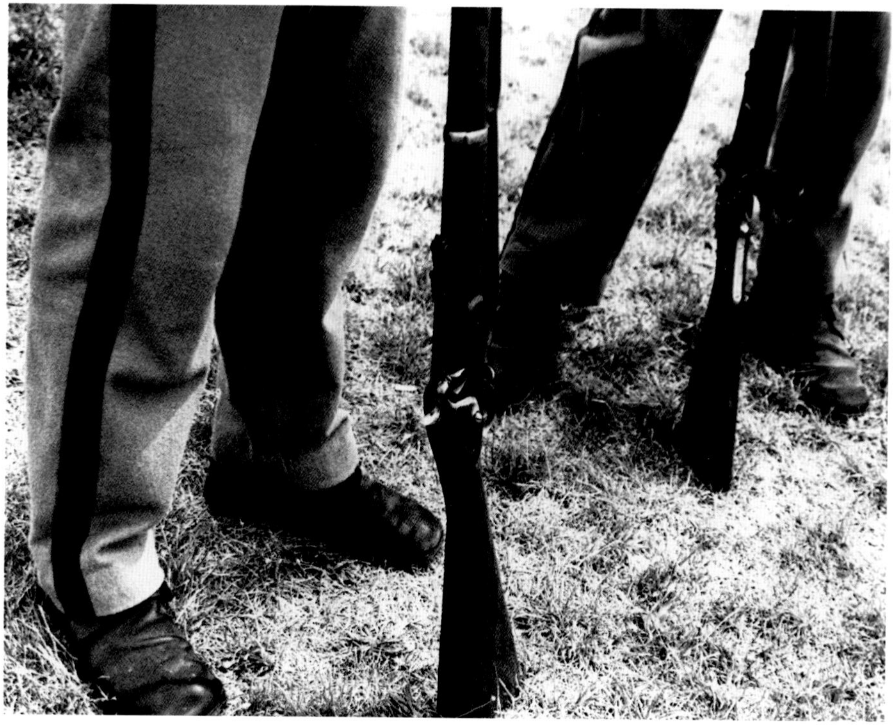

introduction

Antietam, a small winding creek in western Maryland. Sharpsburg, a rural village near Antietam Creek, containing about 700 souls in the waning days of summer in 1862. America's Civil War, our most deadly and destructive conflict, had been raging for over a year with no clear purpose other than restoring the union of the states. With a level of bloodletting unprecedented in American history, the war had already brought sorrow and suffering to thousands of homes North and South.

Abraham Lincoln, a president elected by slightly less than forty percent of the popular vote in 1860, was dedicated to ending what he termed the "rebellion in the Southern states." His call for 75,000 volunteers had driven another four of the slave states to join those seven originally seceding from the Union. In September of 1862, with a failed Union campaign against Richmond and a resurgent Confederate offensive in Tennessee and Mississippi, General Robert E. Lee led a battered but defiant rebel army into Maryland in a bold effort to end the war with an independent Confederacy and a brokered peace.

Although reduced in numbers, uniforms and equipment, Lee's Army of the Northern Virginia was determined to strike a blow that would dishearten and demoralize northern war supporters and possibly elect a pro-peace Congress in November of 1862. Southern hopes for Maryland's support kindled enthusiasm for the invasion, and Confederate President Jefferson Davis anxiously awaited news that Lee had been successful in this first "invasion" of Northern territory. Much was riding on the backs of Lee's weary and footsore patriots, and they slogged on in resolute stoicism to which they had become inured through hard marching and Spartan conditions. It was possible in September of 1862 that Southern hopes might be realized and that ragged band might win the war for the roughly 9 million people residing in the Confederacy.

To halt this campaign and end the hopes of Southern independence,

Union President Abraham Lincoln reluctantly turned to General George B. McClellan. Although regarded as a political rival and chronic complainer, McClellan was the perfect general to reorganize an army and create order out of the chaos of a defeated Union force. Fresh from the Battle of Second Manasass, they streamed in defeat into the nation's capitol and despite the opposition of much of Lincoln's cabinet, McClellan resumed command of the Army of the Potomac. In short order, McClellan organized a field army to pursue Lee's bold adventure into Maryland.

McClellan's first concern was to prevent Lee's ability to move against the cities of Washington D.C. and Baltimore, his second to drive Lee's army from Maryland. Leading a scratch force out of Washington to oppose Lee's army, McClellan moved cautiously towards Frederick, the pivot point of the campaign to this date.

Lee's battered army was resting in Frederick when he received word that a Union base at Harpers Ferry had not evacuated as expected. Dividing his army into five columns to eliminate this threat, the Confederates departed Frederick on September 10th and surrounded the beleaguered Union garrison by September 13th. A bombardment soon commenced, the Union commander having few options but to fight it out.

While the action at Harpers Ferry was taking place, an abandoned Confederate camp yielded a misplaced Confederate order detailing the plans of Lee and his subordinates. Moving quickly, McClellan sent his Union columns to the passes of South Mountain, hoping to catch a divided rebel army and destroy it. A stiff battle ensued, causing nearly 5,000 casualties combined. More importantly, one pass was captured and the Confederate hold on the other two was tenuous. Lee had little choice but to order a complete retrograde movement to the Virginia shore and gather his army.

On the morning of September 15th as he was near Sharpsburg, Lee received a note from his trusted subordinate Gen. Thomas J. Jackson announcing his opinion that the Union troops at Harpers Ferry would surrender that day. Lee gambled that he could reconstitute his army on the high bluffs of the west bank of Sharpsburg and move northward to Hagerstown before the Federal army would attack him. McClellan moved his forces to the east bank and spent the balance of the 15th and 16th reconnoitering the Confederate position. As the straggling rebels waded the Potomac at Shepherdstown and joined Lee, Union General Joseph Hooker was ordered to cross Antietam Creek and position his First Corps men on Lee's left flank. The stage was set for the greatest single day battle of the Civil War, and perhaps the most decisive engagement of the war as well.

Wednesday, September 17, 1862, dawned as a dreary, damp day, a slight rain ending as the sun rose over South Mountain. Hooker's blue-coated soldiers shook off the morning chill and stepped out onto the Miller Farm. A field of corn, surrounded by a zigzag rail fence, was the only visual barrier to conceal the Confederates awaiting the Union assault. In the vicinity of the Miller cornfield that morning, 17,000 Federal troops engaged in a whirlwind of bloody conflict with 11,800 Confederates. In slightly less than three hours of fighting both sides lost over 4,000 men, killed, wounded or missing. Charge and countercharges, desperate fighting and horrific casualties left the landscape littered with he debris of battle, both inanimate and human. Hooker's men were supported by Gen. Joseph Mansfield's Twelfth Corps, but were driven back by repeated attacks by Confederates commanded by Generals J. R. Jones, A. R. Lawton, John B. Hood and Daniel H. Hill.

When it became apparent that this Union drive was stalled, McClellan committed the 15,000 man Second Corps into the fight. Arriving in the East Woods with little knowledge of the situation, their commander, Gen. Edwin V.

Sumner launched a division of 5,000 men to sweep the rebel forces out of the West Woods and from the field. Reacting to the renewed Union drive, 9,000 reinforcements ordered to the area by Lee arrived in the nick of time to catch this Union force on their flank, and drove them back in confusion. The Federals lost over 2,200 men in a few minutes, while Confederate casualties totaled 1,850. This Federal disaster ended serious fighting on this end of the field for the day.

In the center of Lee's defensive line a narrow rutted farm lane was hastily being converted to a bulwark by the remnants of D. H. Hill's division. Sweeping through the burning Samuel Mumma farmstead and across William Roulette's farm were 4,500 men of General William French's Union division of the Second Corps. French ordered his men forward in three successive lines against the well-placed Southerners. Three times the Federals advanced; and three times they were thrown back. The last second Corps division arrived and added their weight to the attack. General Meagher's Irish brigade approached to within 100 yards of the sunken road and blazed away at the Confederates sheltered by the fence rails and dirt. General Richard Anderson's Confederates came up from the reserve to help Hill, but were swept away by Federal fire. After a fight that raged for two-and-a-half hours, the Federal troops flanked the rebel troops and drove them from the lane. Leaving 2,600 of their comrades dead or wounded, the surviving Confederates retreated across Henry Piper's farm, pausing to stand at the stone walls lining the Hagerstown Pike. Although it seemed that the Federals might continue the assault, confusion and casualties halted the Union troops and allowed the Confederates a reprieve. Federal losses of nearly 3,000 men discouraged a renewal of offensive operations.

There was a perceived opportunity for Union troops to drive in the center of Lee's lines towards the middle of the day, a concerted effort by the Fifth and Ninth Corps may well have ended the day with a decisive Union triumph. The chance was never taken; McClellan still was convinced he faced a superior Confederate force and did not order the advance. With a stalemate in place in the northern and center parts of the field, all hope Federal success now focused on the small stone-arched bridge over Antietam Creek located on the southern part of the field.

General Ambrose Burnside was ordered to seize the bridge that now bears his name and strike towards the town of Sharpsburg and Lee's escape route over the Potomac. Only a handful of Georgian troops held the high ground on the west side of the creek. Taking advantage of the natural cover, they provided a stalwart and stubborn defense of the span. Attacks by the Ninth Corps against the well-placed began around 10:00 in the morning, and after several failed efforts, a gallant charge by two regiments, coupled with a flanking movement downstream, forced the Confederate soldiers to retreat back towards their comrades on the ridge to the rear. Federal soldiers poured across the bridge and a massive assault was organized to drive Lee's battered defenders from their last position. Nearly 9,000 Union men advanced across the fields south of Sharpsburg, driving the vastly outnumbered Southerners before them. Just when it appeared that the demise of Lee's army was at hand, the last Confederate troops arrived on the field. After an exhausting march from Harpers Ferry, General A. P. Hill led his division onto the field and into the flank of the Federal advance. Surprised and confused, Union soldiers recoiled from this attack, falling back to the bridge and holding their ground there.

As the shadows of evening grew and the guns fell silent, many survivors of this awful day of carnage took stock of the field. Thousands of men lay dead, and thousands more dying or grievously wounded. Fences, farms, and fields were shattered and destroyed. Almost every building in Sharpsburg was damaged; several were burning. Shocked civilians emerging from basements and nearby caves were horrified at the wholesale destruction of both life and property. As night fell the weak-beamed lanterns appeared to mark the people searching for wounded comrades on the gruesomely littered battlefield.

It is impossible to say with certainty the number of men whose lives were forever altered by the events of September 17, 1862. Over 3,600 men were killed outright during the battle. Over 17,000 were wounded; many of them eventually died of those wounds. Another 1,800 were missing, their fates uncertain. Defying these finite numbers are the memories of the survivors who endured incredible hardship and suffering on that awful day. From the day of the battle to decades later the men who stood in battle that day always recalled Antietam as a horrific experience.

The Southerners retreated back to Virginia on September 19th, leaving the field and victory to the Union army. McClellan's forces remained to recuperate and guard the Potomac frontier. Lee's plans for southern independence in the fall of 1862 were dashed and President Lincoln used this victory to announce his Emancipation Proclamation. The high tide of the Confederacy had crested at Sharpsburg, and receded only to lap again against the bulwark of the Union. The war would grind on for another two-and-a-half years. Thousands more would suffer death or wounds, but the end would not come until the spring of 1865.

Dr. Thomas G. Clemens, historian, President, Save Historic Antietam Foundation

The enchantment of a photograph is only marginally about what is captured through the lens of a camera. The true magic of a photograph lies in what cannot be seen - as in life - *still life.*

H. Casser-Jayne

the photographs

"As we stood looking upon that brilliant pageant, I thought, if I did not say, 'What a pity to spoil with bullets such a scene of martial beauty!' But there was nothing else to do. Mars is not an aesthetic God, and he was directing every part of the game in which giants were contestants."

Colonel John B. Gordon
6th Alabama Infantry
Rodes' Brigade

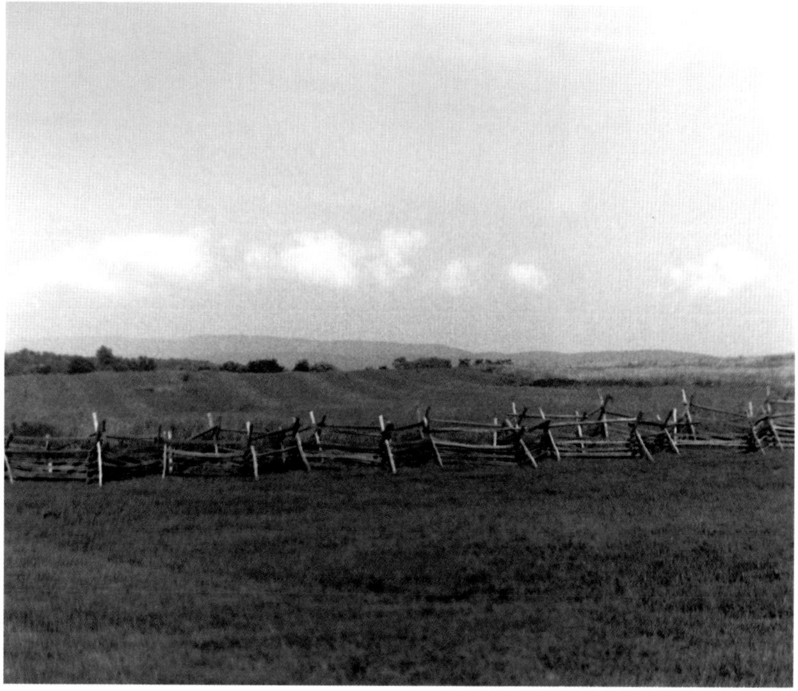

"The Chaplain had no appointment or recognized place on a march, in a bivouac, or in a line of battle; he was a supernumerary, a kind of fifth wheel to a coach, being in place nowhere and out of place everywhere."

Frederic Denison
Rhode Island Cleric

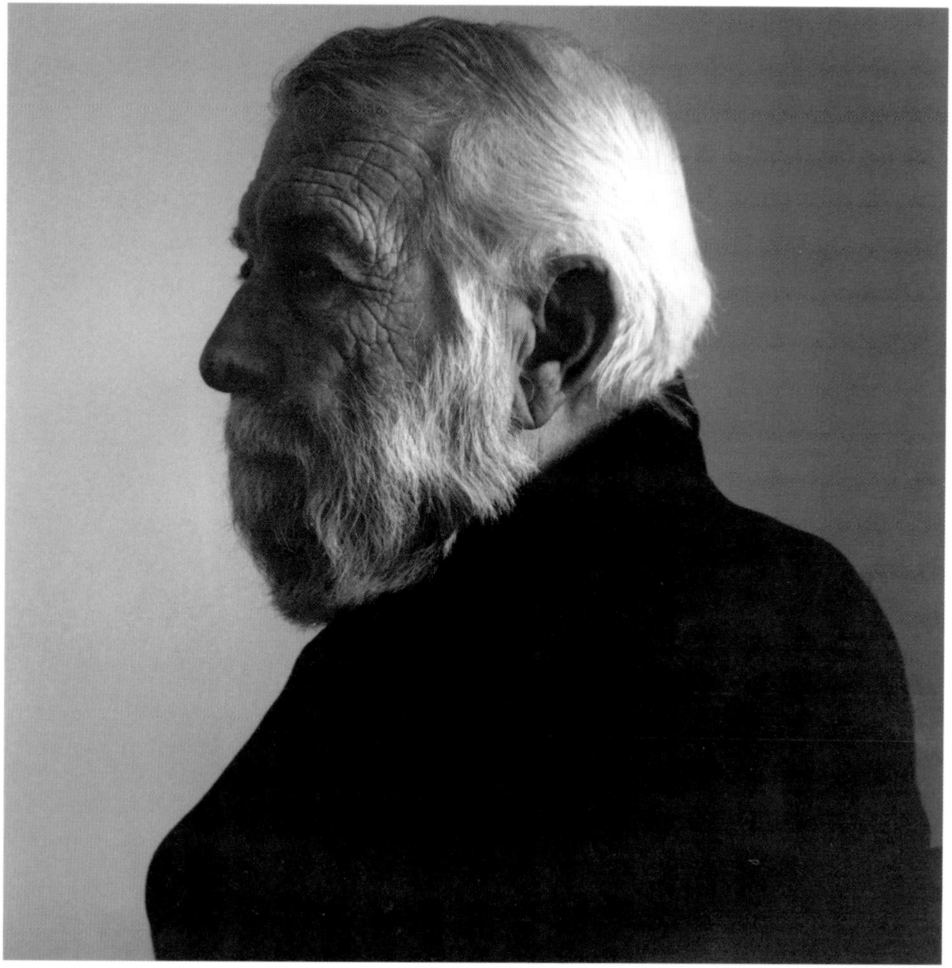

"Whatever may be the result of the contest, I foresee that the country will have to pass through a terrible ordeal, a necessary expiation, perhaps, of our national sins."

General Robert E. Lee
5 May 1861
letter to "My dear Little H–," a Northern girl

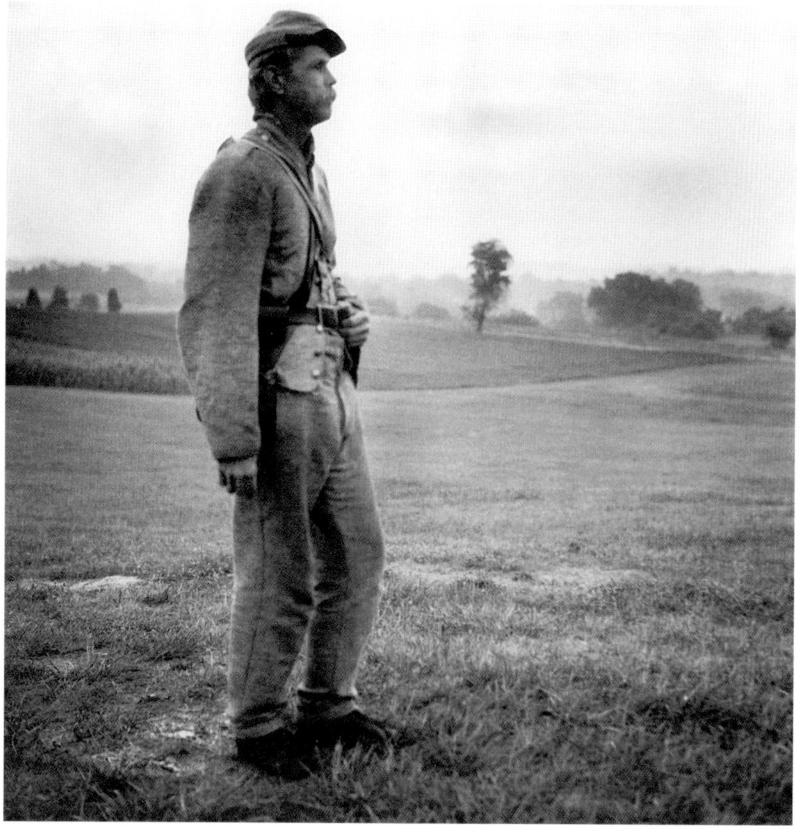

"McClellan declared that he could now, 'cut the enemy in two and beat him in detail.'"

Following the receipt of Lee's military plan
Special Order 191
Issued September 9, 1862

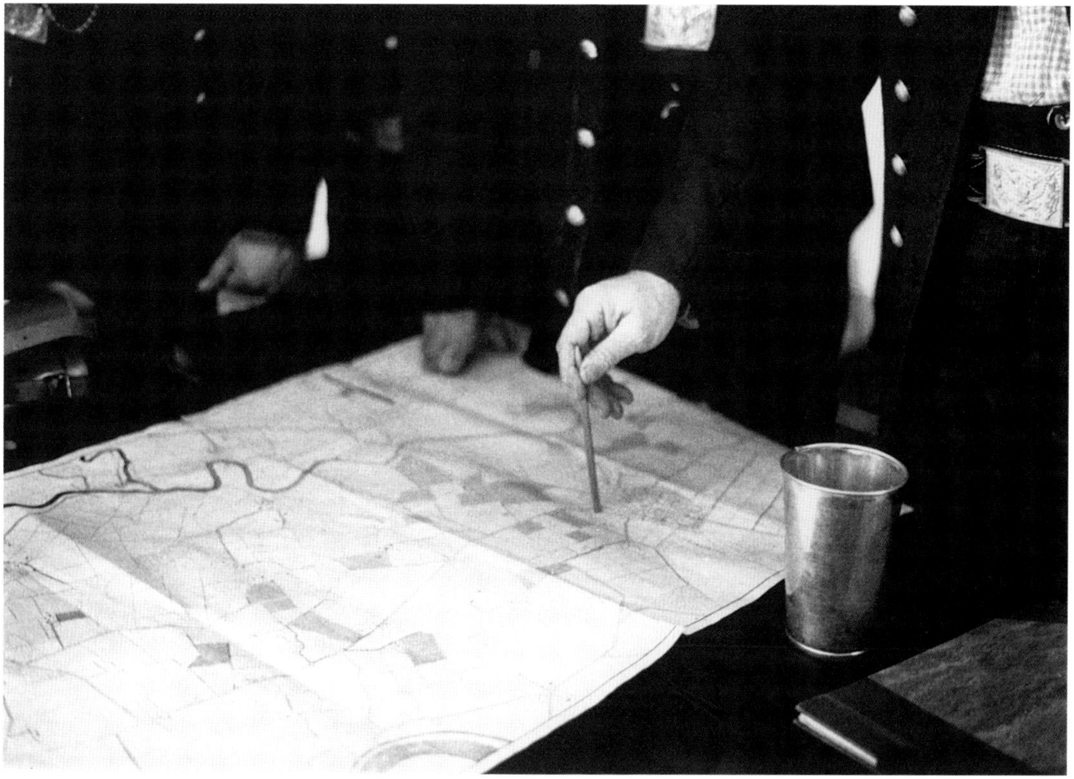

"To mass troops against the fire of a covered line is simply to devote them to destruction. The greater the mass, the greater the loss - that is all."

Union General John. M. Schofield

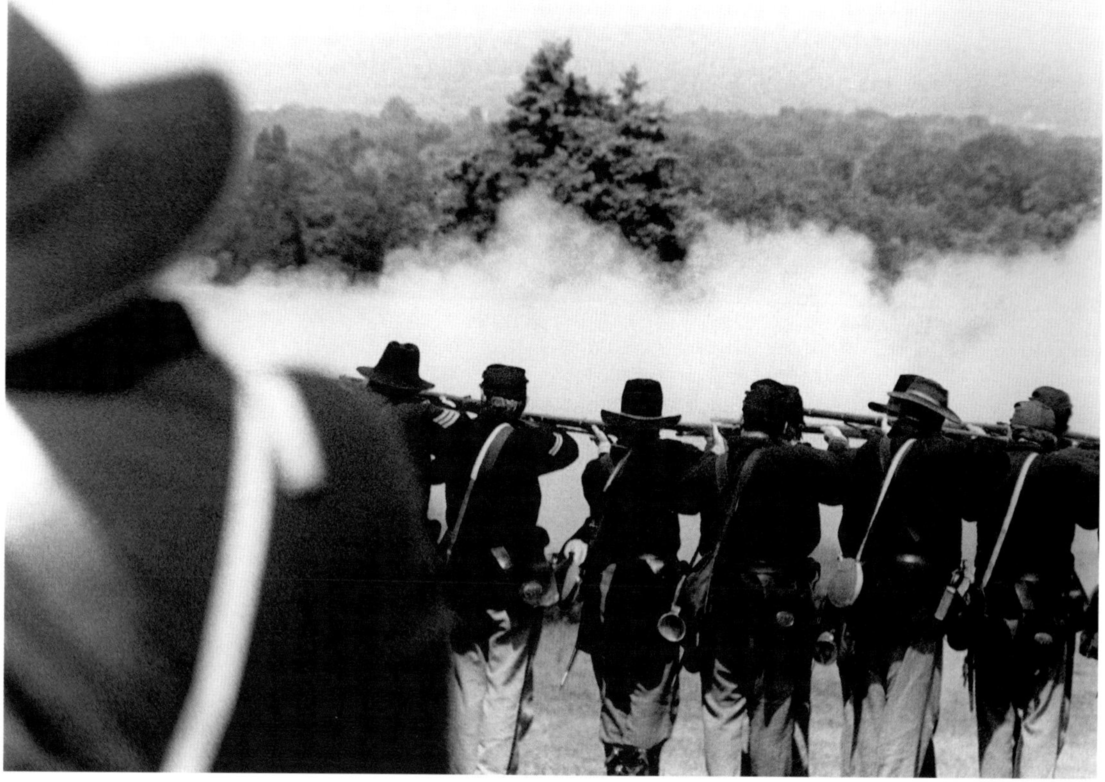

"The sun went down; the thunder died away, the musketry ceased, bivouac fires gleamed out as if a great city had lighted its lamps."

Charles Carleton Coffin
War Correspondent

"I said to him it was a very dangerous place, so near the colors. He said, 'Yes, everywhere is dangerous here.'"

Corporal John T. Parham
32nd Virginia Infantry
Semmes' Brigade

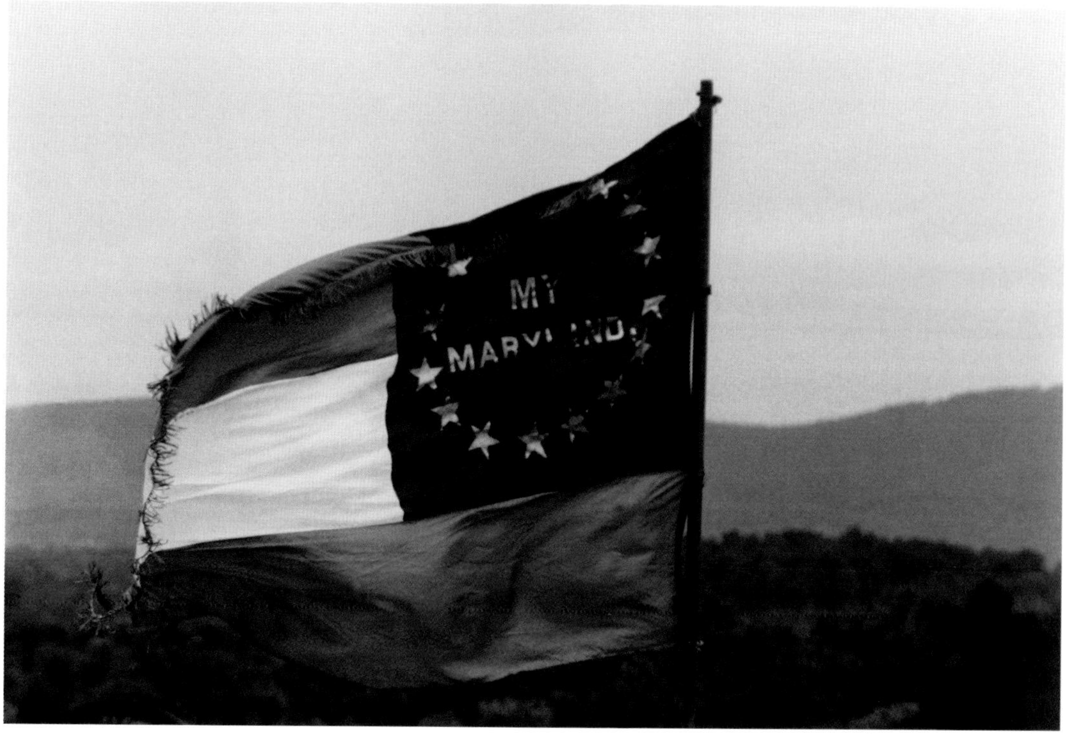
MY

"**Y**ou might as well attempt to put out the flames of a burning house with a squirt-gun. I think this is to be a long war - very long - much longer than any politician thinks."

William Tecumseh Sherman

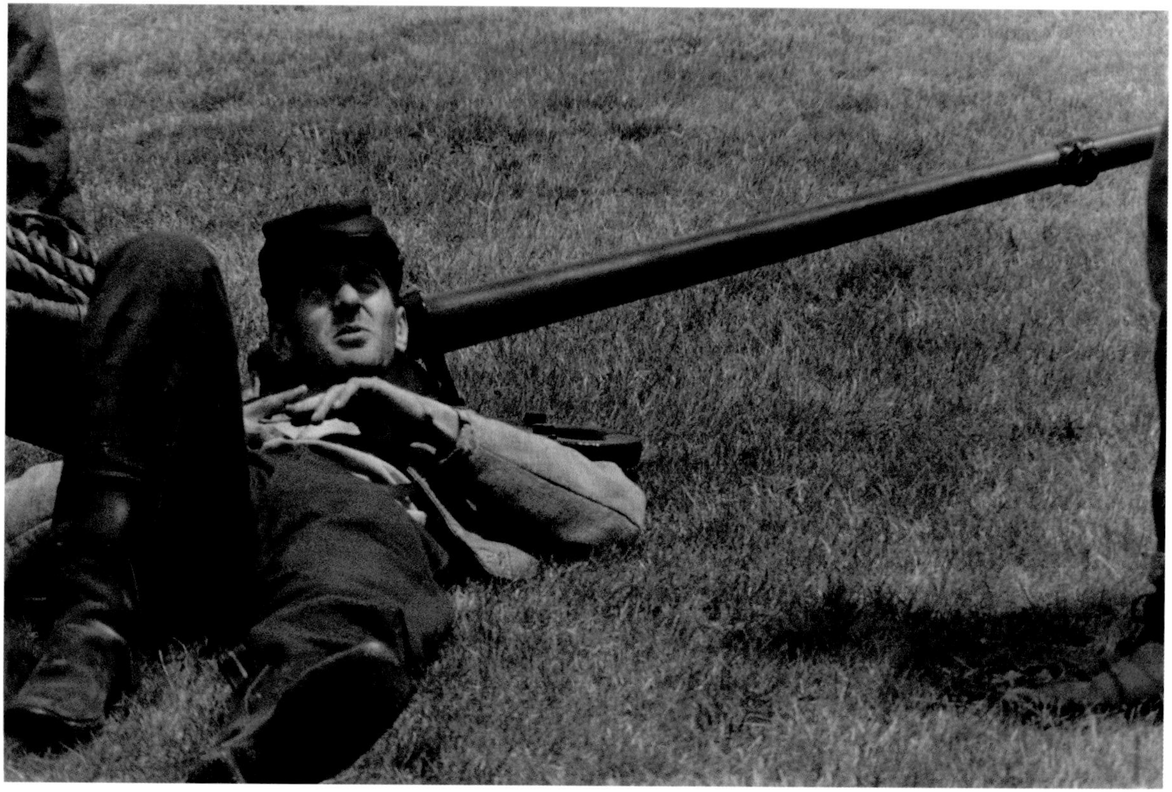

"When we came to that beautiful cornfield, boys, that's when the trouble began."

Private J. Polk Racine
5th Maryland (U.S.) Infantry
Weber's Brigade

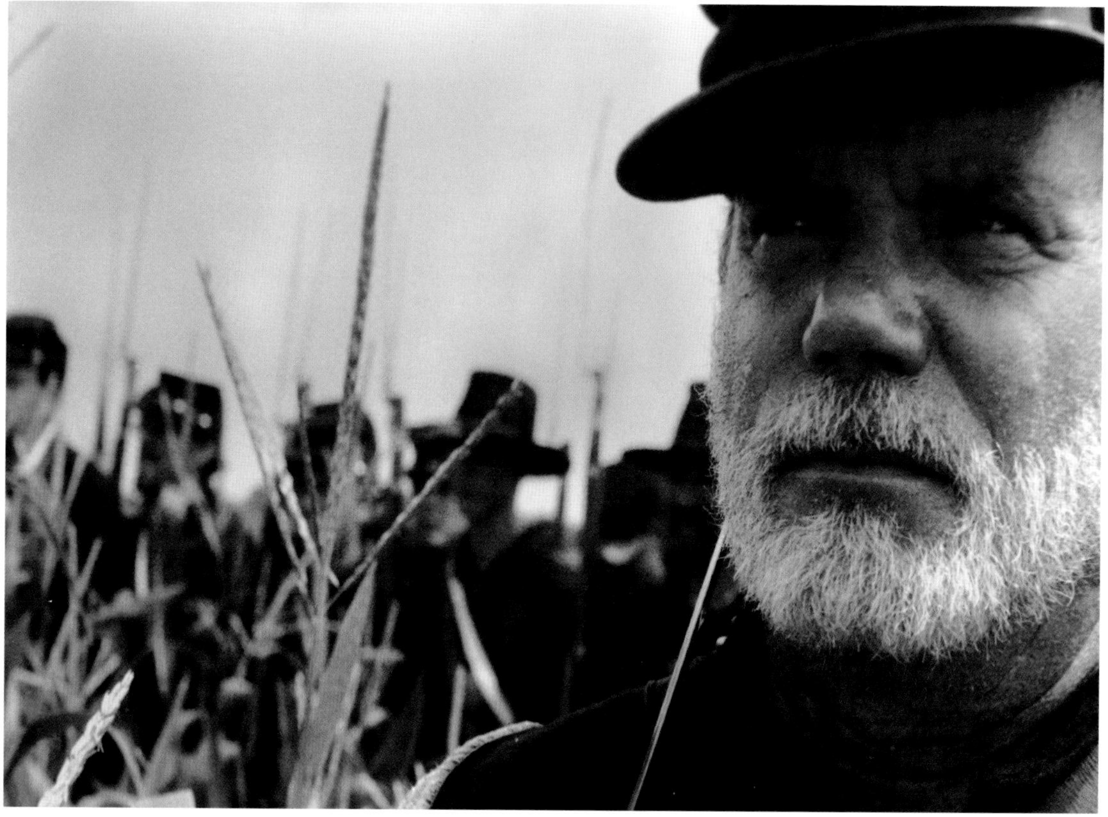

"Then for the first time I saw the carnage of battle, men lying in every conceivable shape, and mangled in a horrible way; but this did not make a particle of impression on me, but horses running around riderless with blood streaming from their nostrils, lying on the ground hitched to guns gnawing their sides to death."

28 July 1861
William Tecumseh Sherman
letter to his wife following 1st Bull Run

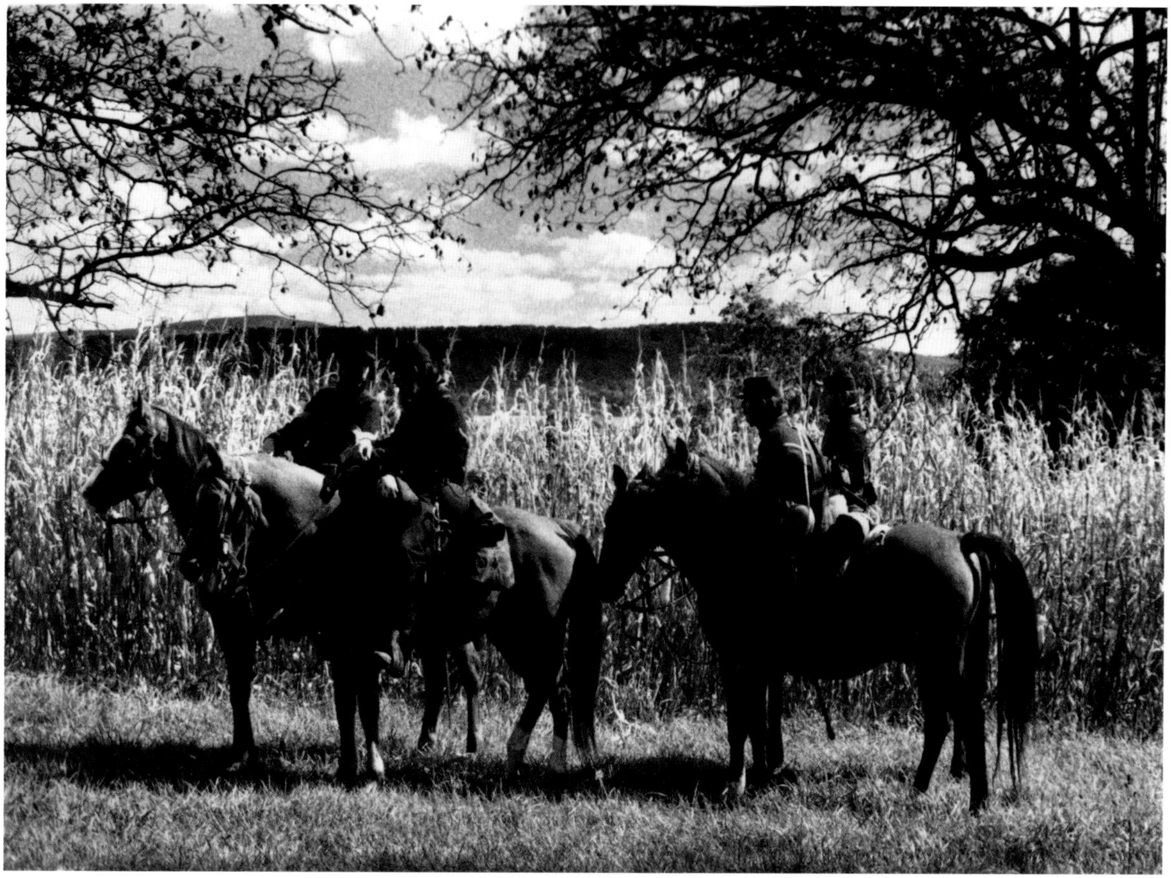

"The despot's heel is on thy shore,
Maryland!
His torch is at thy Temple door,
Maryland!
Avenge the patriotic gore
That flecked the streets of Baltimore.
And be the battle Queen of your,
Maryland! My Maryland!"

James Ryder Randall
26 April 1861
Maryland! My Maryland!

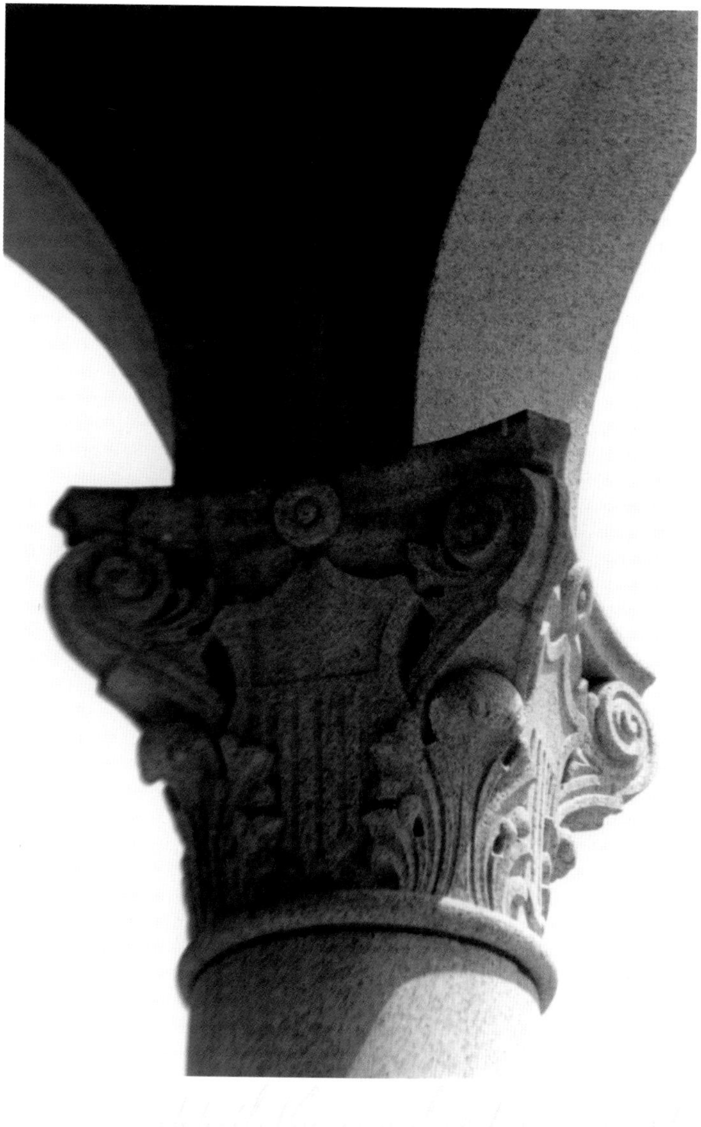

"Another day's march brought us to Hagerstown where the cornfields and orchards furnished our meals. The situation, in a sanitary point, was deplorable. Hardly a soldier had a whole pair of shoes. Many were absolutely bare-footed, and refused to go to the rear. The ambulances were filled with the foot-sore and sick."

Pvt. Alexander Hunter
Company A
17th Virginia Infantry

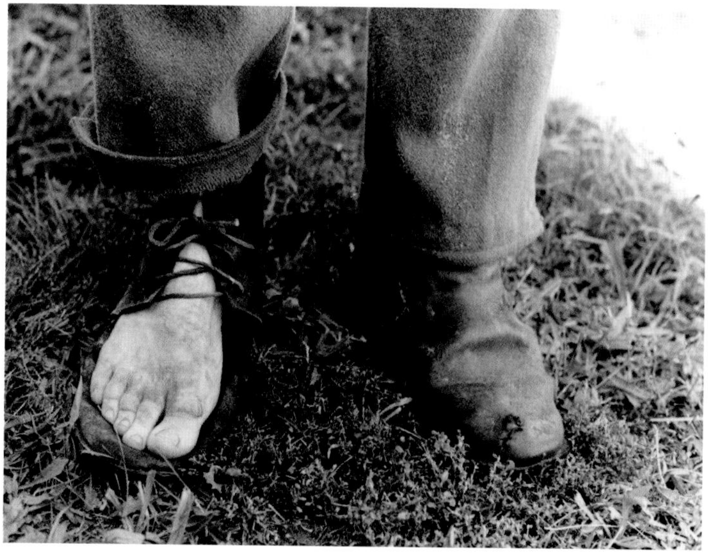

"Our names would go resounding down the corridors of time, our deeds be perpetuated in song and story."

Private Otis D. Smith
6th Alabama Infantry
Rhodes' Brigade

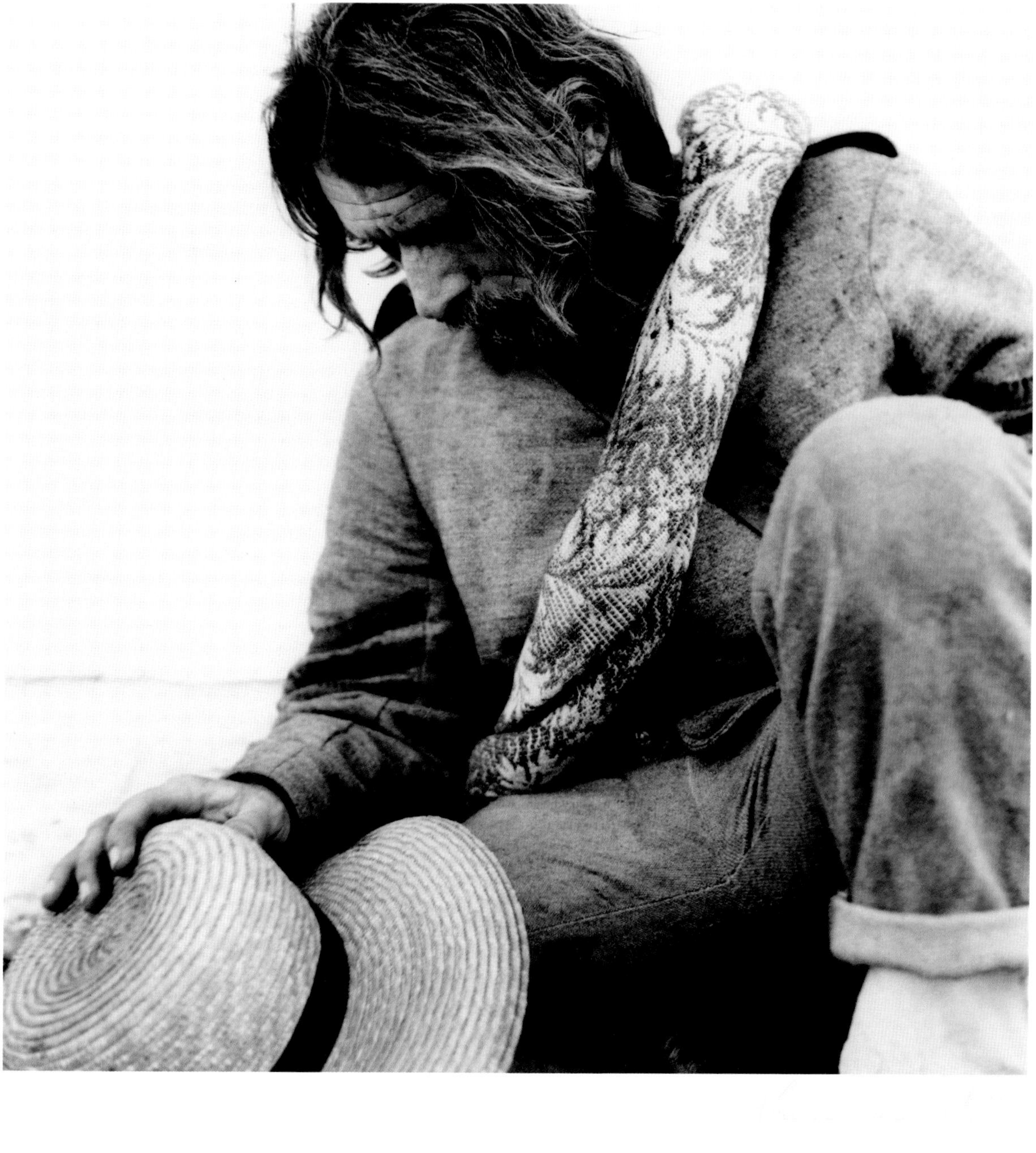

"We discovered last week a soldier who turned out to be a girl. She had already been in service for 21 months and was twice wounded. Maybe she would have remained undiscovered for a long time if she hadn't fainted. She was given a warm bath which gave the secret away."

Fanny J. Anderson
editor, *The Shelley Papers*

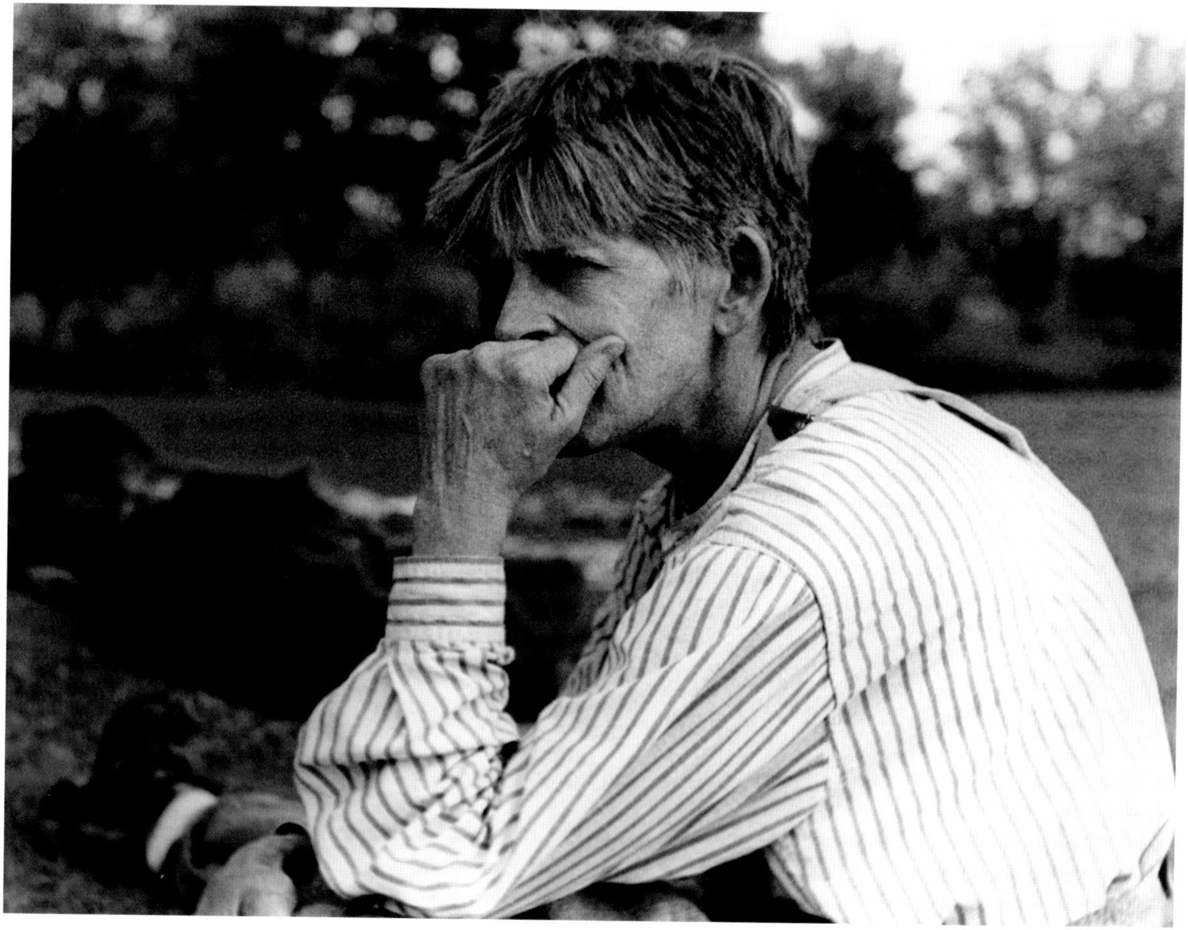

"Every button must be in place and buttoned, every bit of metal polished bright, every gun as clean clear to the bottom of the bore as it could be made, every stitch sewed, every particle of dust absent, every strap in place, every man clean, every one's hair short and combed, every shoe blacked clear around the heels, every knapsack packed with a clean change of underclothes, and every cartridge, cap, and primer in its place."

Sergeant Thomas Livermore
5th New Hampshire

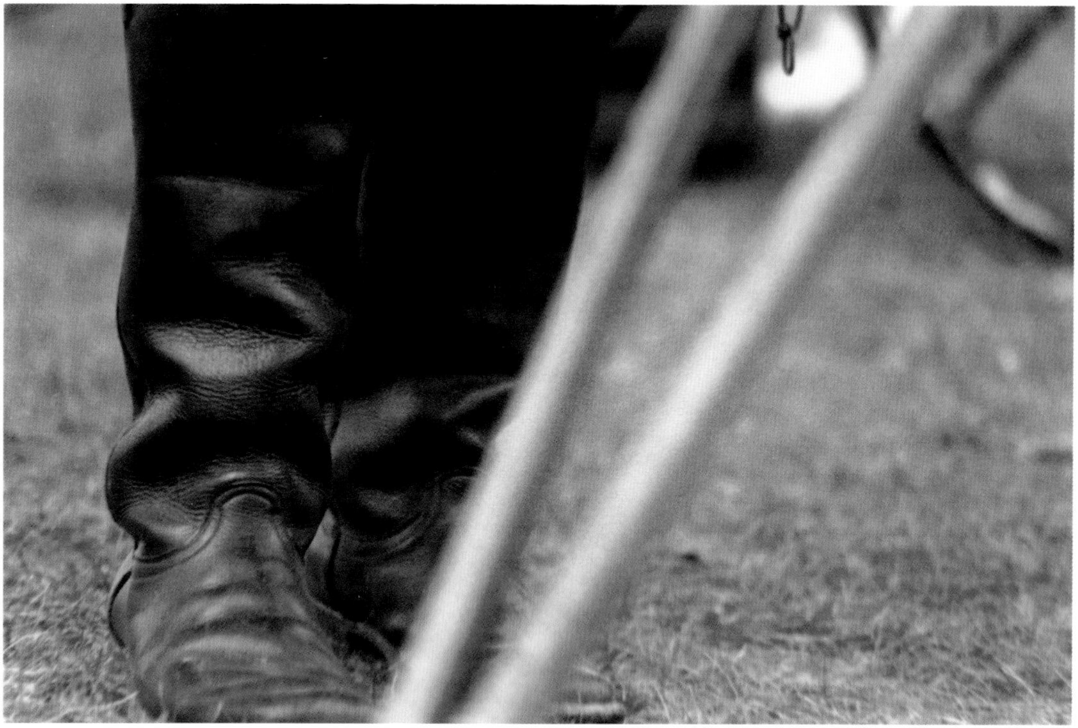

"During the brief half hour to forty minute struggle around the Dunker Church, casualties soared. The 7th South Carolina lost one hundred forty of two hundred sixty-eight engaged...The Federals suffered as terribly. The 111th Pennsylvania lost one hundred ten of three hundred present. The Confederates took out two hundred sixty-eight effectives of the 28th Pennsylvania. The 125th Pennsylvania counted two hundred twenty-nine casualties of about 700 engaged... The Federals lost approximately thirteen men per minute in the assault on the Dunker Church."

Unknown

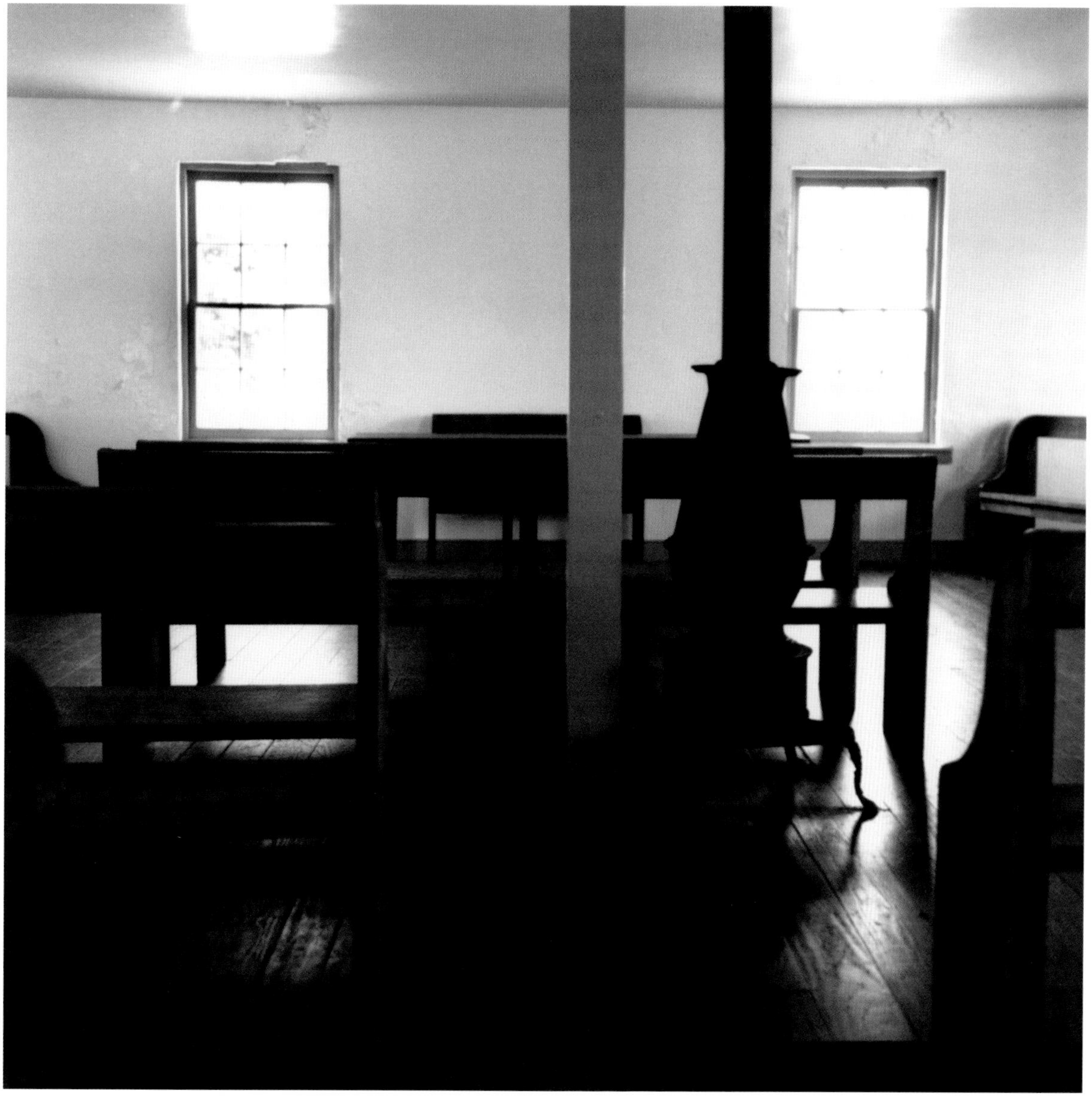

"We're tenting tonight
on the old camp ground
Give us a song to cheer
Our weary hearts, a song of home
And friends we love so dear.
Many are the hearts that are weary tonight,
Wishing for the war to cease;
Many are the hearts that are
Looking for the right
To see the dawn of peace.
Tenting tonight, Tenting tonight,
Tenting on the old Camp ground."

Tenting On the Old Campground
Walter Kitridge
1863

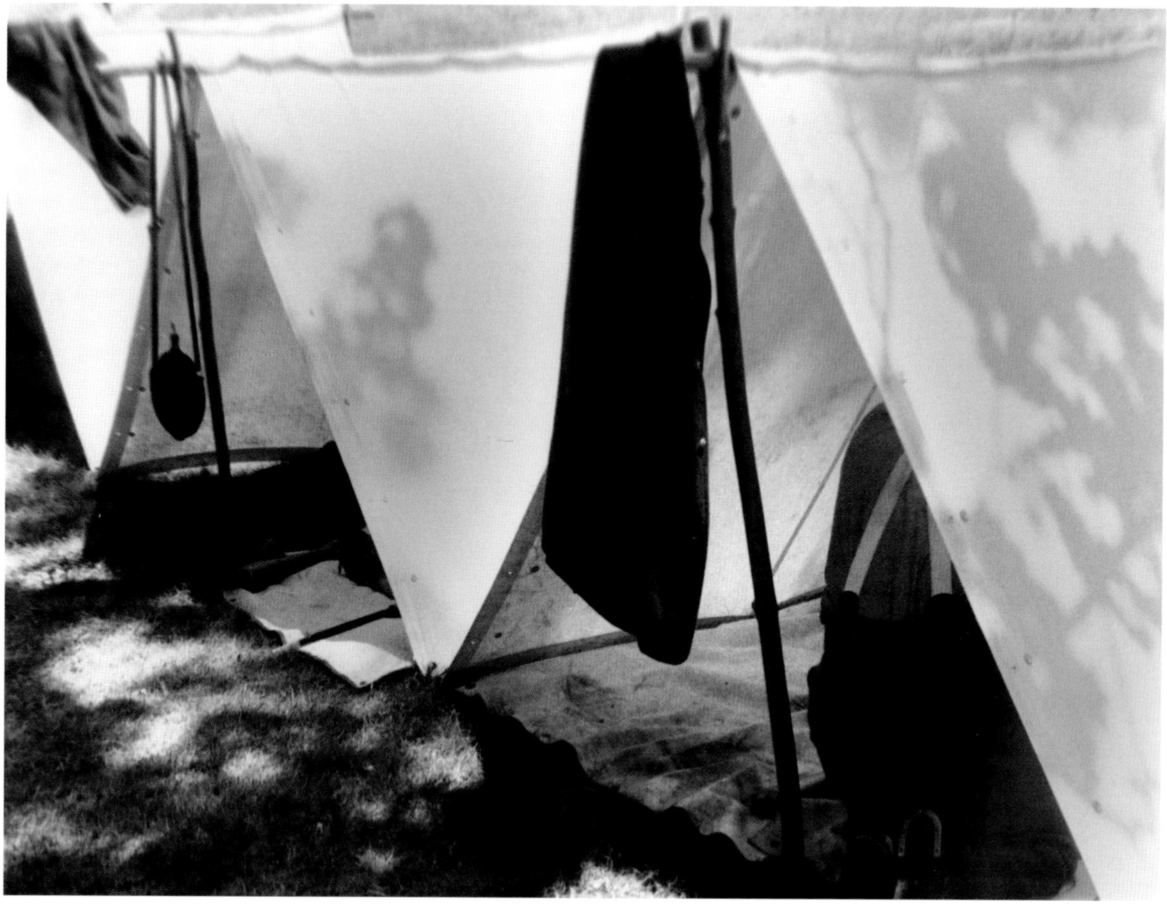

"Every gun fired in this struggle, no matter on which side, no matter what else it hits or misses, lodges a ball in the carcase of the writhing monster. Man may hesitate or vacillate, but the judgement of God is sure, and under that judgement Slavery reels to its certain downfall."

New York Times
20 May 1862

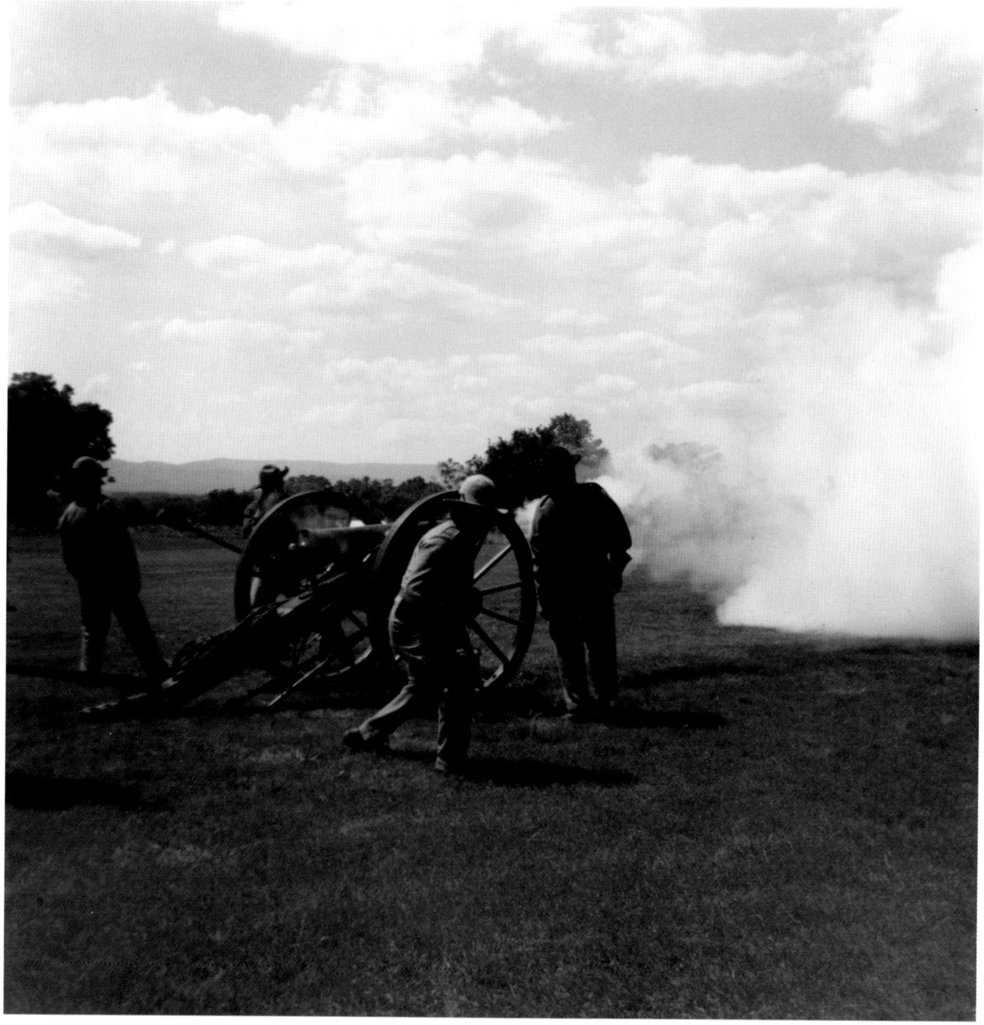

"War is an organized bore."

Captain Oliver Wendell Holmes, Jr.
20th Massachusetts Infantry

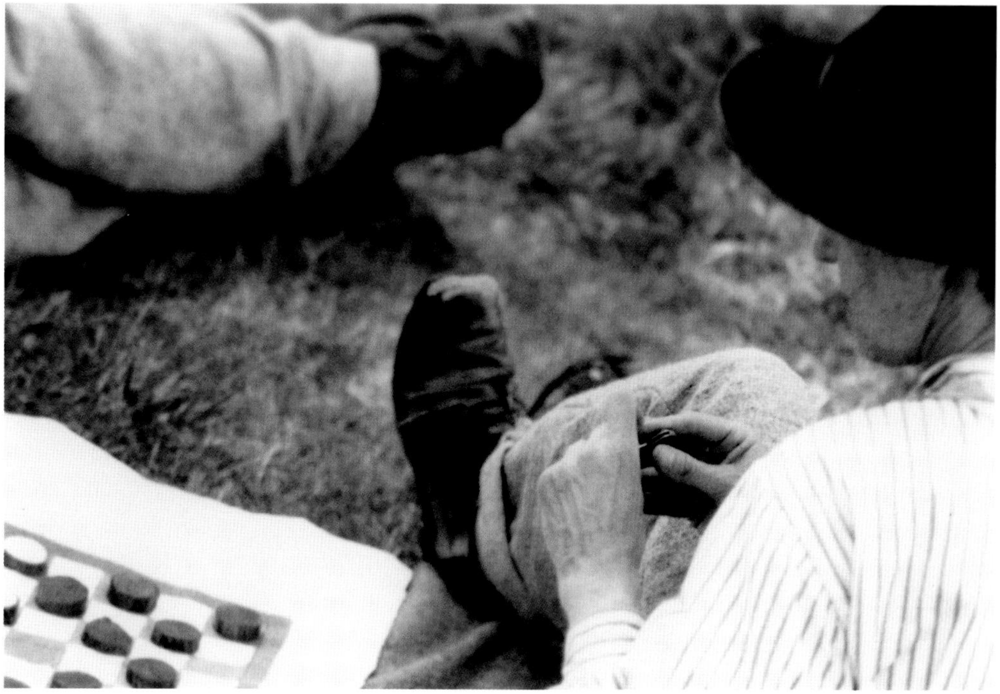

"After all a little spice of danger, every day, is an excellent thing; it drives away the blues and gives to the soldier's life that dash of romance which makes pictures on the memory that never fade."

Major James Austin Connolly
9 December 1863
from a letter to his wife

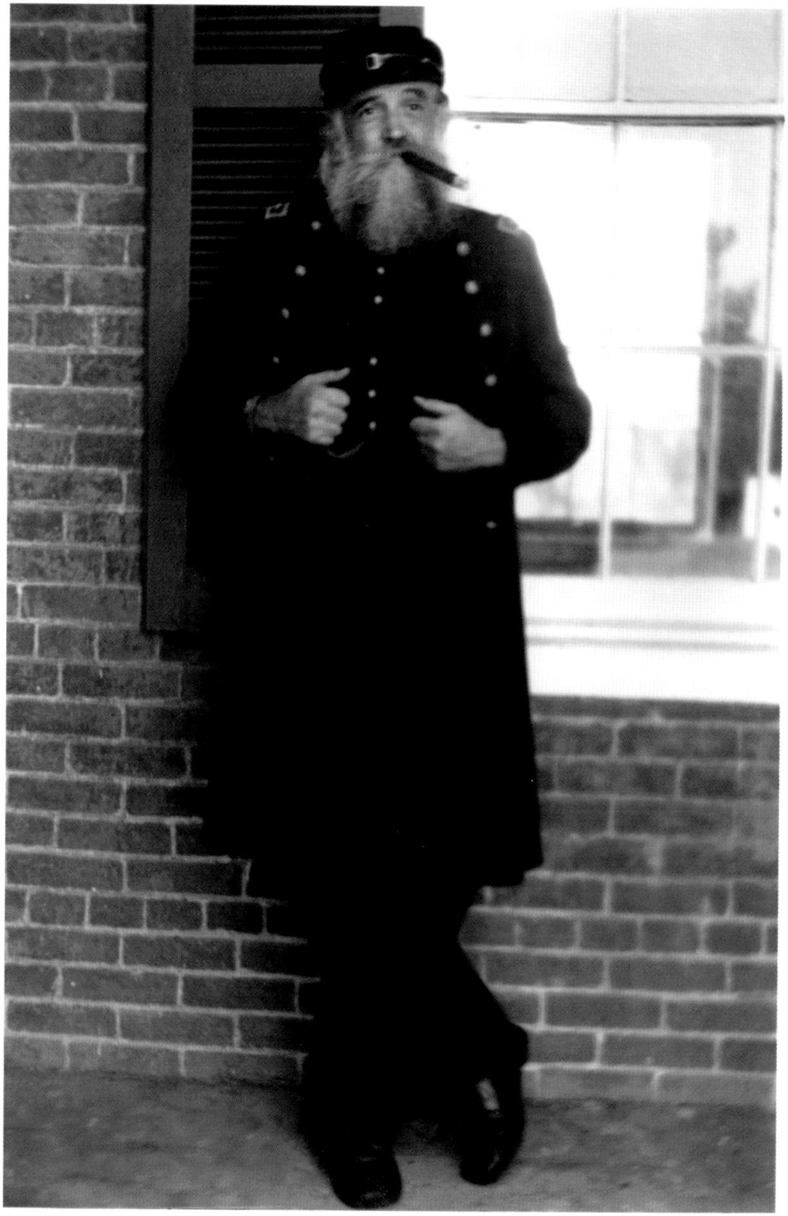

"I recall a remarkable scene. The sun was going down, - its disc red and large as seen through the murky battle-cloud. One of Sumner's batteries was directly in line toward the sun, on the crest of the ridge north of the smoking ruins of Mumma's house and barn, and there was one piece of which the gunners, as they rammed home the cartridge, seemed to be standing in the sun. Beyond, hid from view by the distance and the low-hanging branches of the oaks by Dunker Church, the Confederate's guns were flashing. Immediately north of Sharpsburg, and along the hill in front, now the National Cemetery, Longstreet's cannon were in play. Halfway up the hill were Burnside's men sending out a continuous flame, with A. P. Hill's veterans confronting them. All the country was flaming and smoking; shells were bursting above the contending lines..."

Charles Carleton Coffin
Army Correspondent

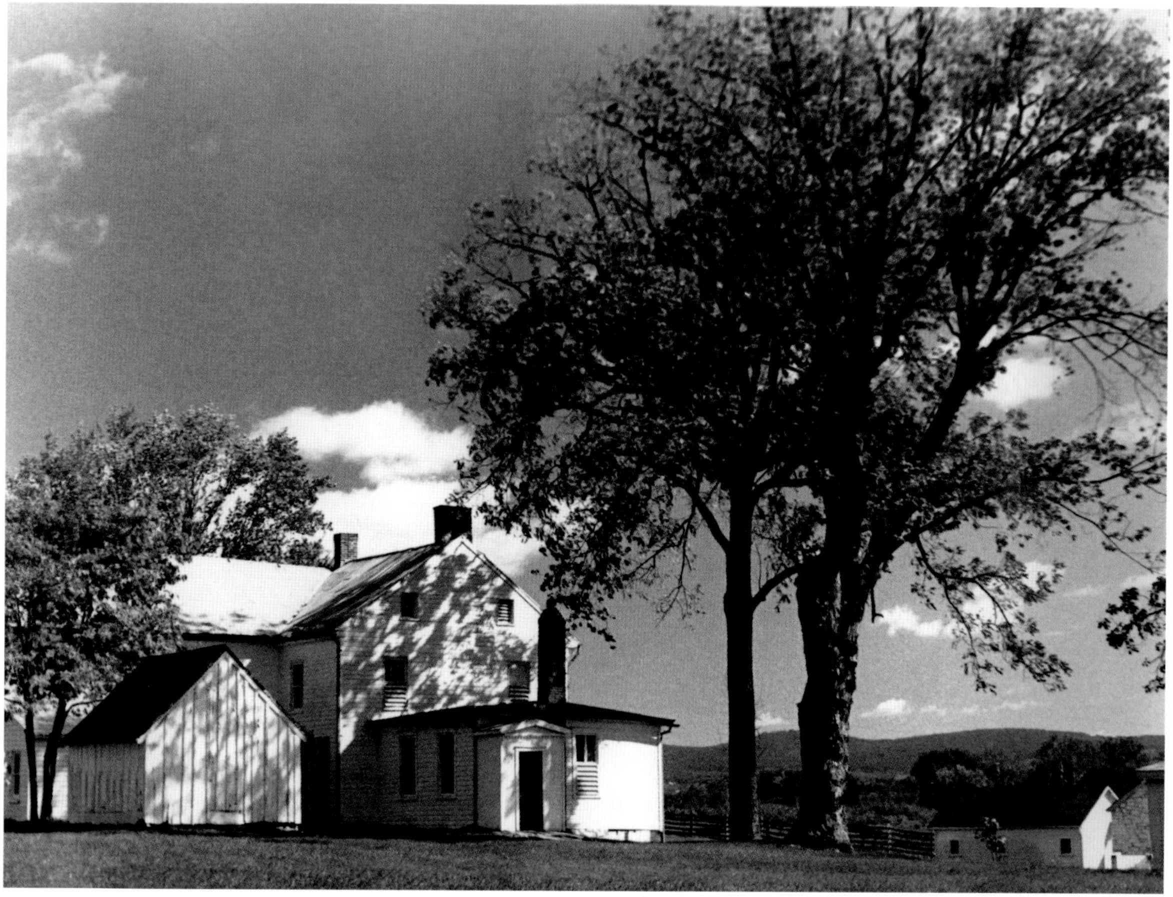

"It was upon the women that the greatest burden of this horrid war fell. While the men were carried away with the drunkenness of the war, she dwelt in the stillness of her desolate home..."

Colonel James Nisbet
who commanded a regiment of Georgians
a remark following the war

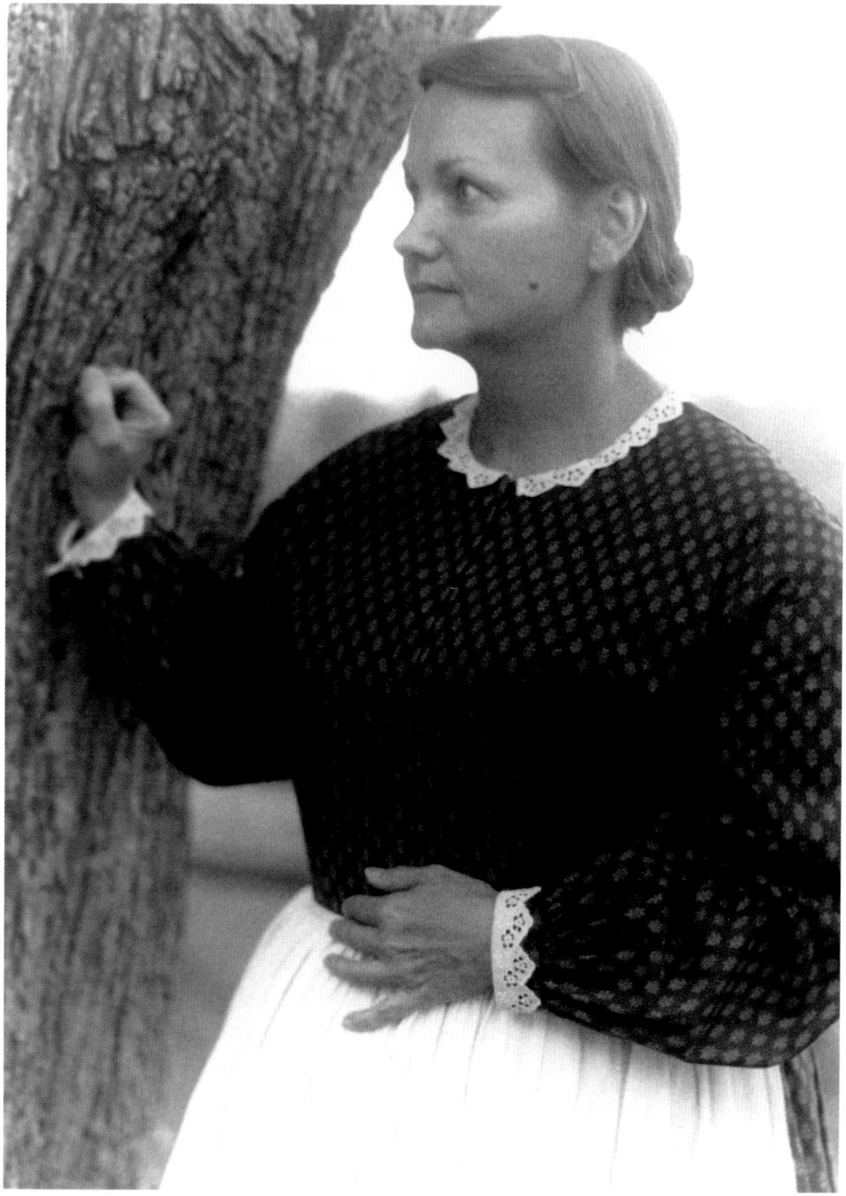

"They were the embodiment of manhood; men who neither toils and sufferings, nor the fact of death, nor disaster, nor hopelessness could bend from the resolve."

Brevet Major General Joshua L. Chamberlain
United States Army

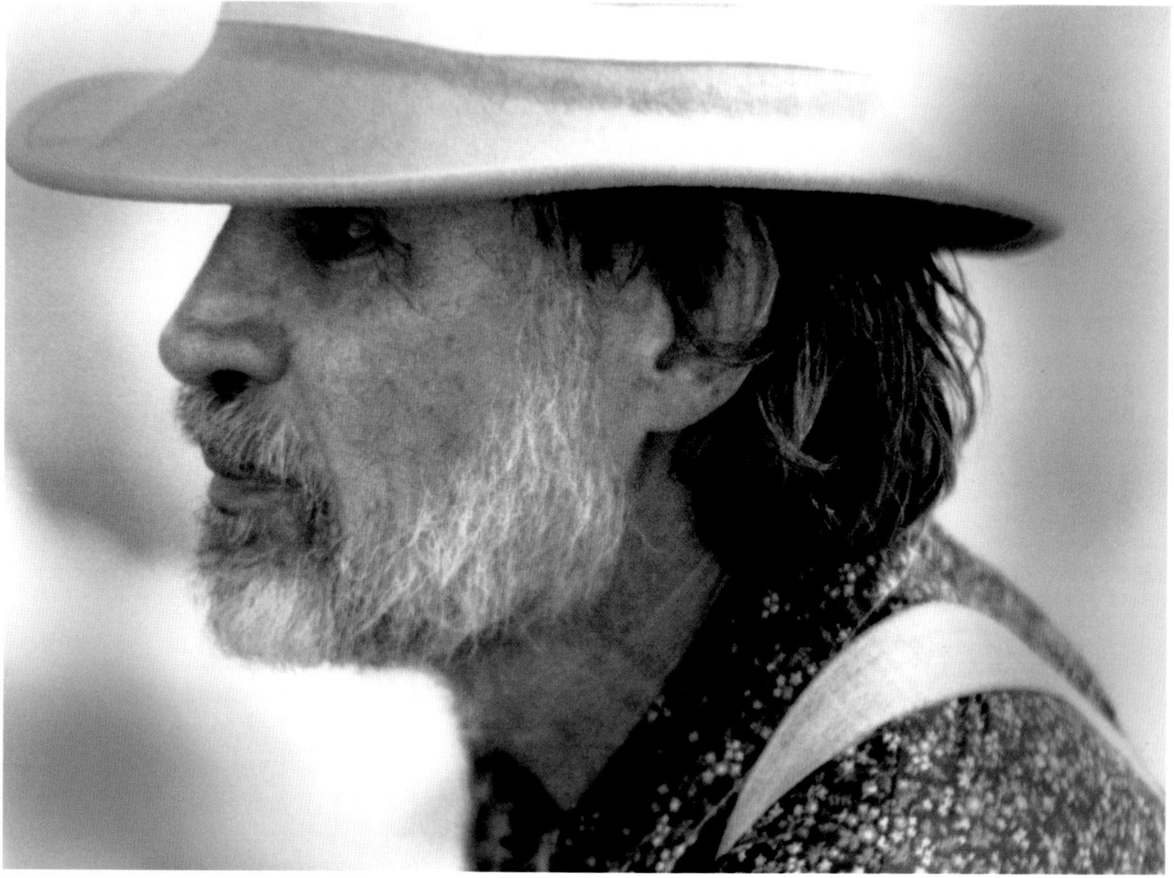

Antietam

"On the afternoon of the 15th, the blue uniforms of the Federals appeared among the trees that crowned the heights on the eastern bank of the Antietam. The number increased, and larger and larger grew the field of the blue until it seemed to stretch as far as the eye could see, and from the tops of the mountains down to the edges of the stream gathered the great army of McClellan."

Lt. General James Longstreet, CSA
Commander, Longstreet's Corps
Army of Northern Virginia

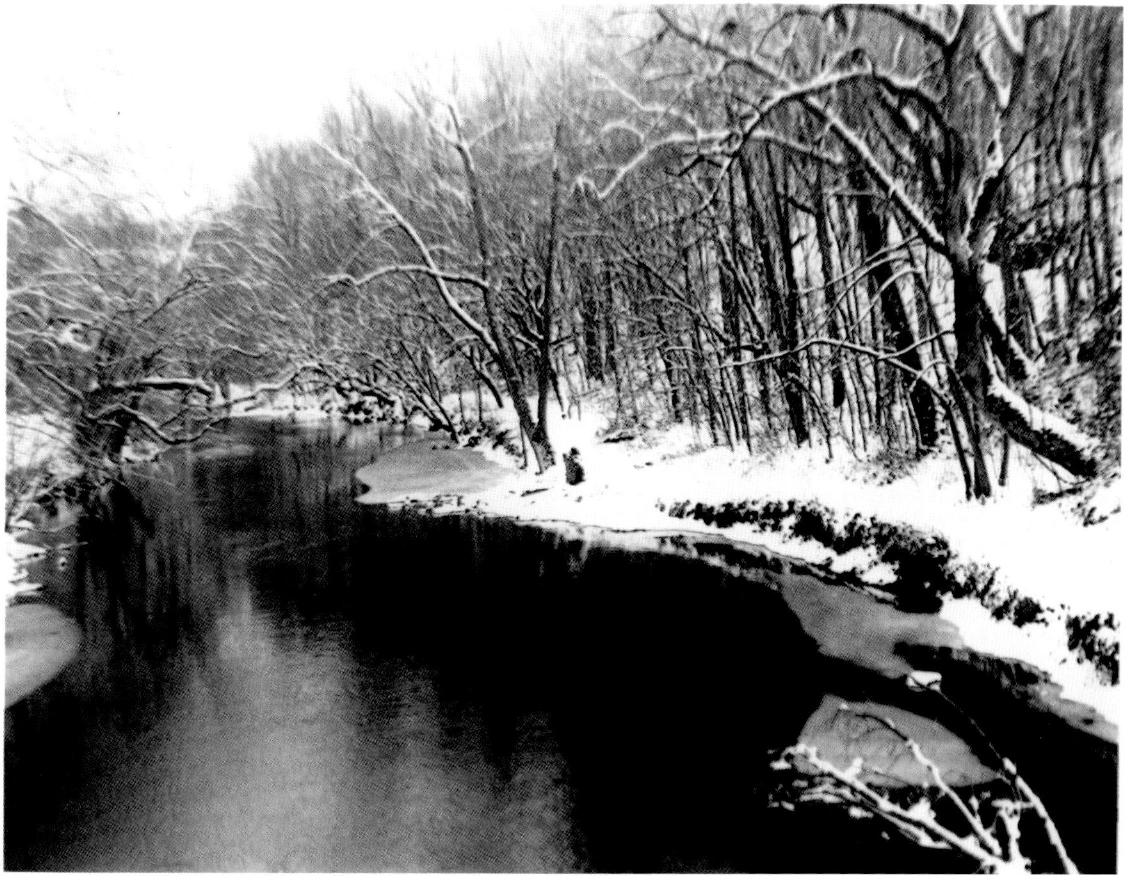

"I have often longed to see a war, and now I have my wish. I long to be a man; but as I can't fight, I will content myself with working for those who can."

Louisa May Alcott, author
from her journal
April 1861

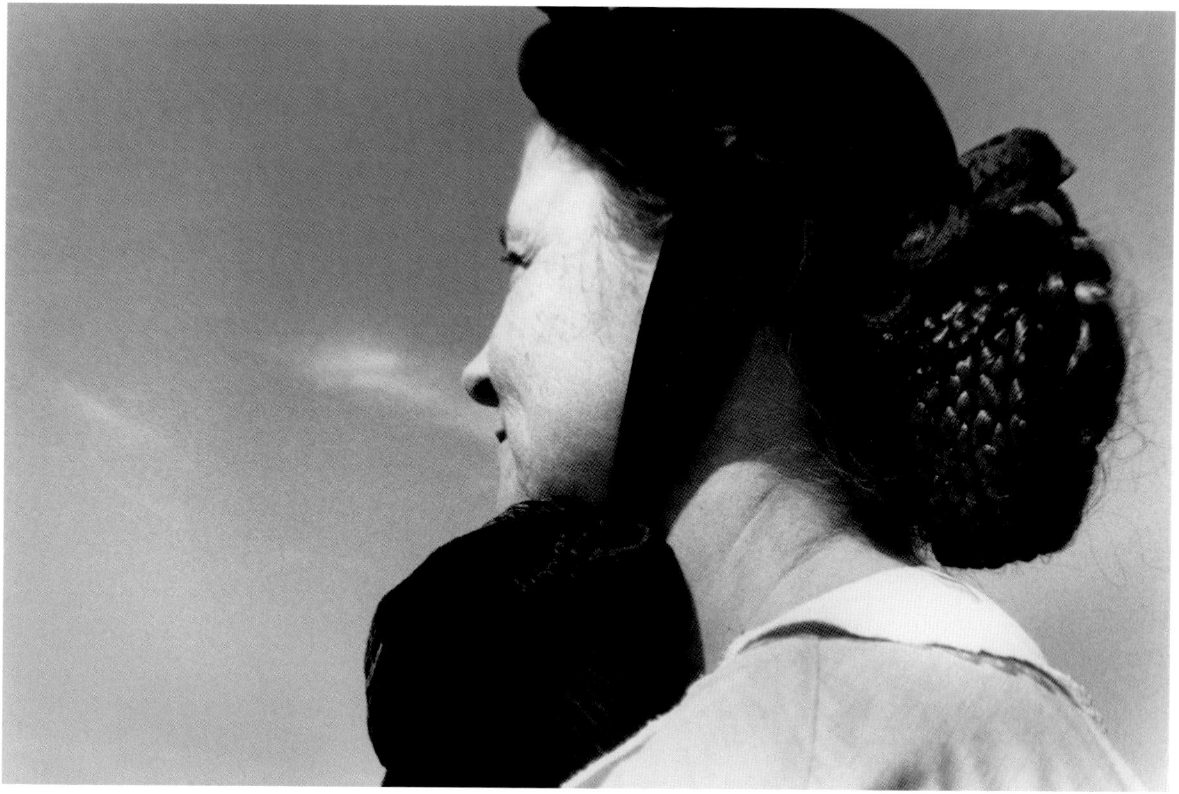

"While passing along a worm fence, in the darkness, we heard a feeble voice almost under our horses' feet." 'Don't let your horses t-r-e-a-d on m-e!' "We at once pulled up, and peering over the pommels of our saddles into the darkness, we could distinguish the dim outlines of a human form extended across our path. Who are you? we inquired." 'I belong to the 20th Mas-sa-chu-setts rig-i-ment,' answered the voice; 'I can't move - I think my back's broken.' "We sent for an ambulence and gave orders to care for the poor fellow, who was one of Sedgwick's men. This was but one of the very many instances of human suffering we encountered that night."

C. S. General Walker

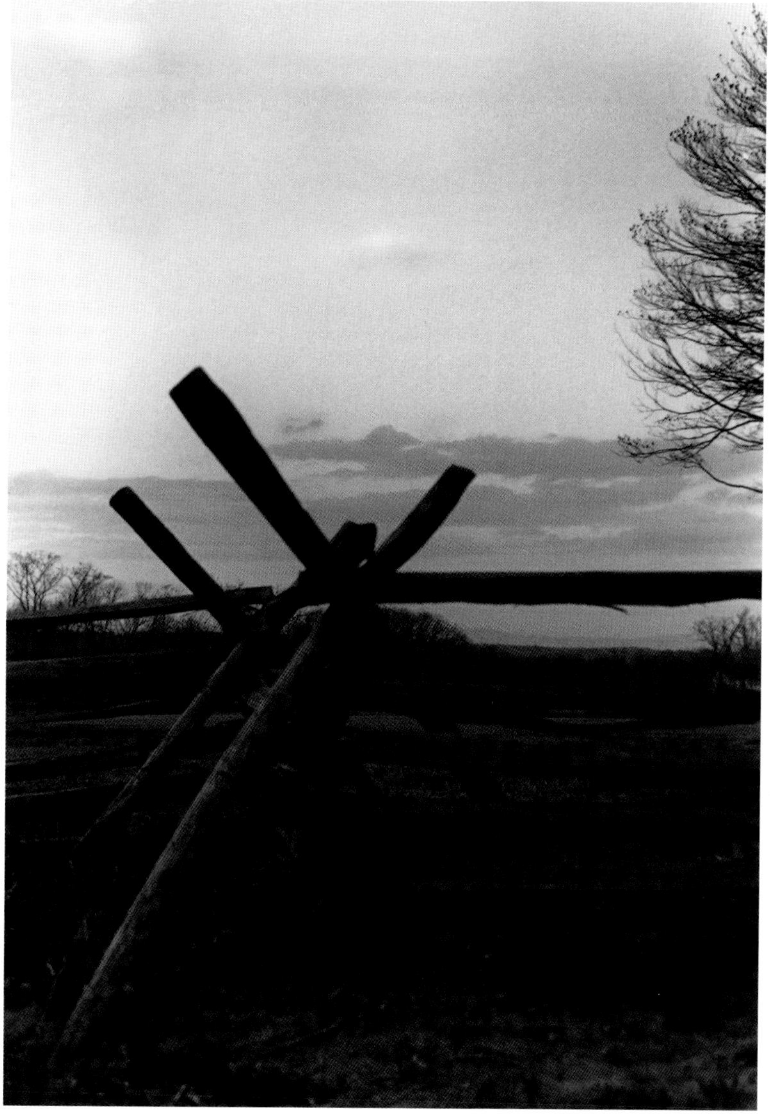

"In the time I am writing every stalk of corn in the northern and greater part of the field was cut as closely as could have been done with a knife, and the slain lay in rows precisely as they stood in their ranks a few moments before. It was never my fortune to witness a more bloody, dismal, battlefield."

Joseph Hooker
USA, Commander 1 Corps
Army of the Potomac

the cornfield

Hero

"**A** hero is no braver than an ordinary man, but he is brave five minutes longer."

Ralph Waldo Emerson

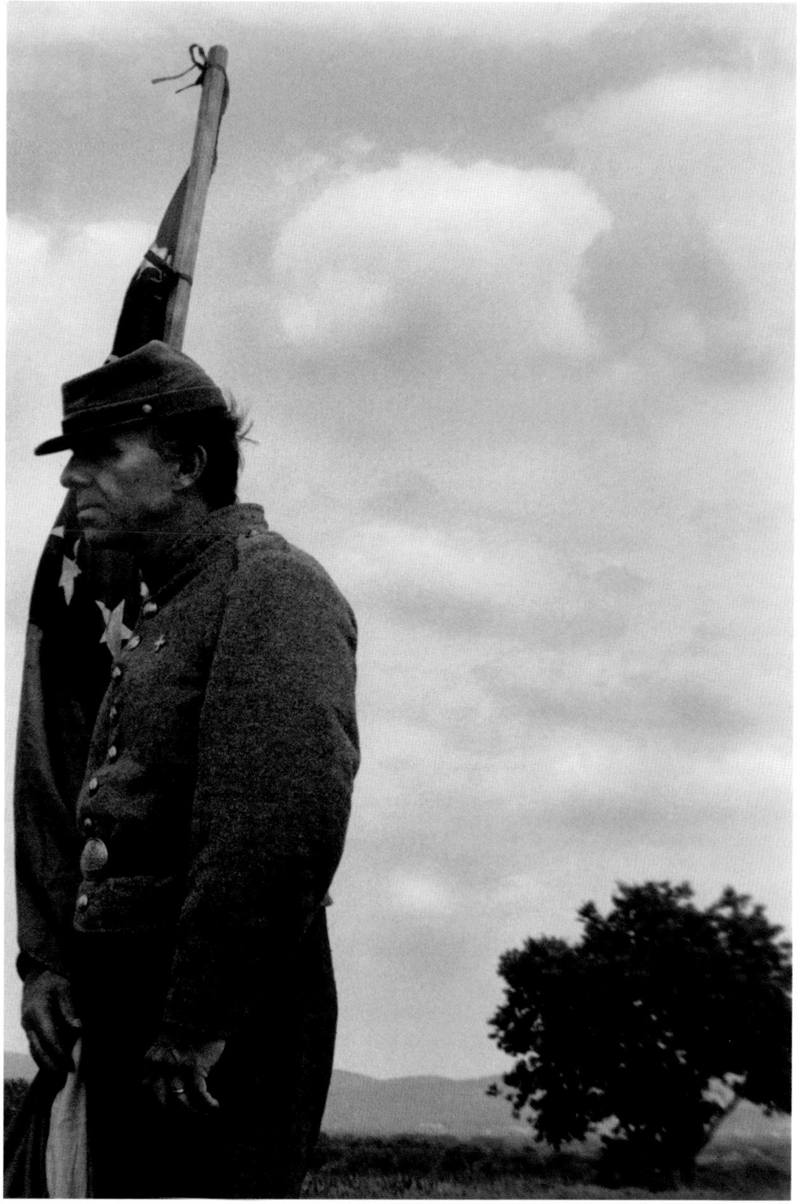

"The battle opened about day-break along the whole line... We advanced steadily upon them, under a heavy fire, and had not gone far when Herod Wilson, of Company F, the bearer of the color, was shot down. Major J. H. Dingle, Jr., then caught them and began to advance with them, exclaiming, "'Legion, follow your colors!' The words had an inspiring effect, and the men rallied bravely under their flag, fighting desperately at every step. He bore the colors to the edge of the corn near the turnpike road, on our left, and while bravely upholding them within 50 yards of the enemy and three Federal flags, was shot dead. I immediately raised the colors and again unfurled them amid the enemy's deadly fire, when Marion Walton, of Company B, volunteered to bear them. I resigned them into his hands, and he carried them gallantly and safely through the battle."

Lieutenant-Colonel M. W. Gary
Hampton's Legion
John B. Hood's Texas Brigade

the monument to the 125th pennsylvania

"I started out this thing a boy; I am now a man."

From a letter to his father
Captain Oliver Wendell Holmes, Jr.

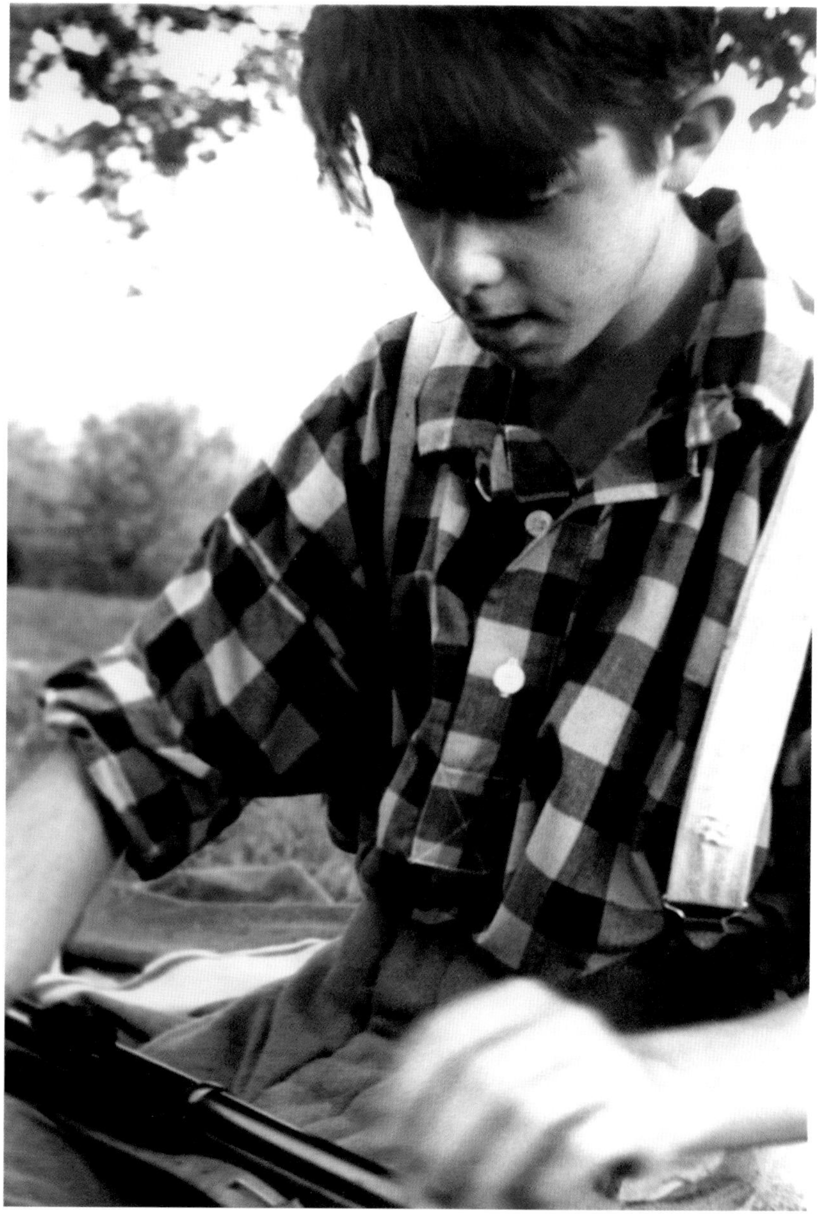

"All were calling for water, of course, but none was to be had. We lay there until dusk — perhaps an hour, when the fighting ceased. During that hour, while the bullets snipped the leaves from a young locust tree growing at the edge of the hollow and powdered us with fragments, we had time to speculate on many things among others, on the impatience with which men clamor, in dull times, to be led into a fight."

David L. Thompson
Company G
9th New York Volunteers

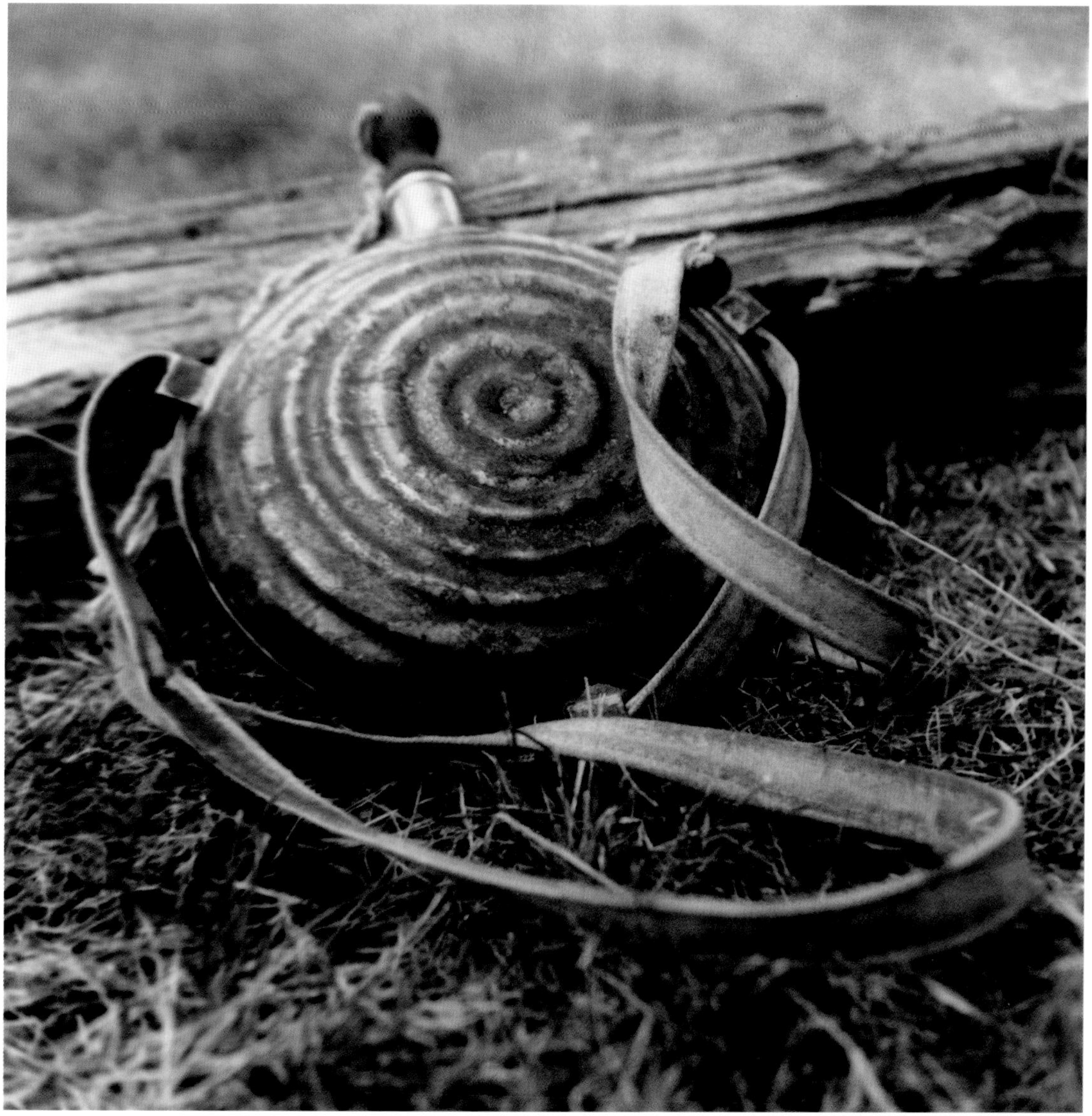

"William Roulette, unaware of whose troops were tramping over his farm, stepped out of his cellar. The moment he recognized a squad from the 14th Connecticut escorting a few more Rebels from his spring house, he went wild." 'Give it to 'em!' "he screamed." 'Drive 'em! Take anything on my place, only drive 'em!' "The last the New Englanders saw of him, he was heading rearward."

Major Frederick L. Hitchcock
132nd Pennsylvania

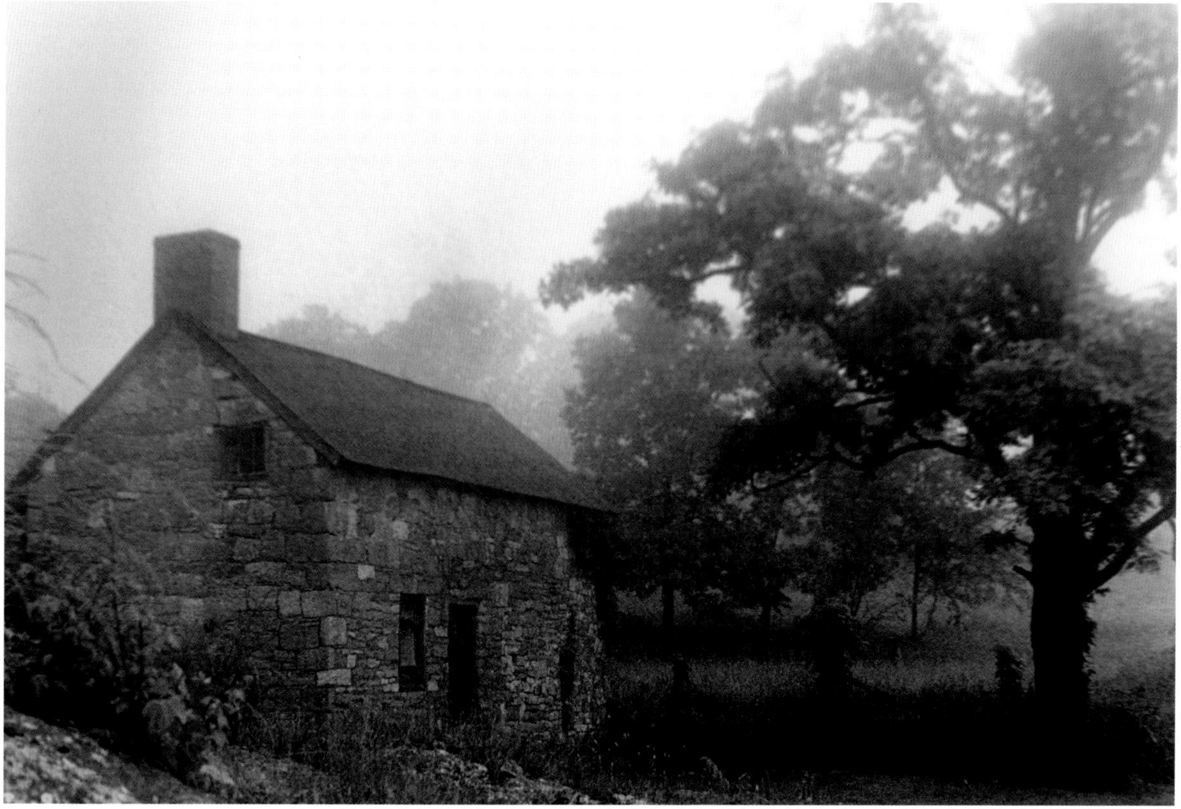

"Both read the same Bible, and pray to the same God; and each invokes His aid against the other. It may seem strange that any men should have to ask a just God's assistance in wringing their bread from the sweat of other men's faces' but let us judge not that we be not judged. The prayers of both could not be answered - that of neither has been answered fully. The Almighty has his own purposes..."

Abraham Lincoln
March 1865
2nd Inaugural Address

"Old Missus marry Will-de-Weaber,
Look away! Look away! Look away!
Dixie Land.
But when he put his arm around her,
He smiled as fierce as a forty-pounder,
Look away! Look away! Look away!
Dixie Land!
Den I wish I were in Dixie, Hoo-ray! Hoo-ray!
In Dixie Land, I'll take my stand to lib and die in Dixie;
Away, away, away down south in Dixie,
Away, away, away down south in Dixie."

I Wish I Were in Dixie Land
Daniel Decatur Emmett
1859

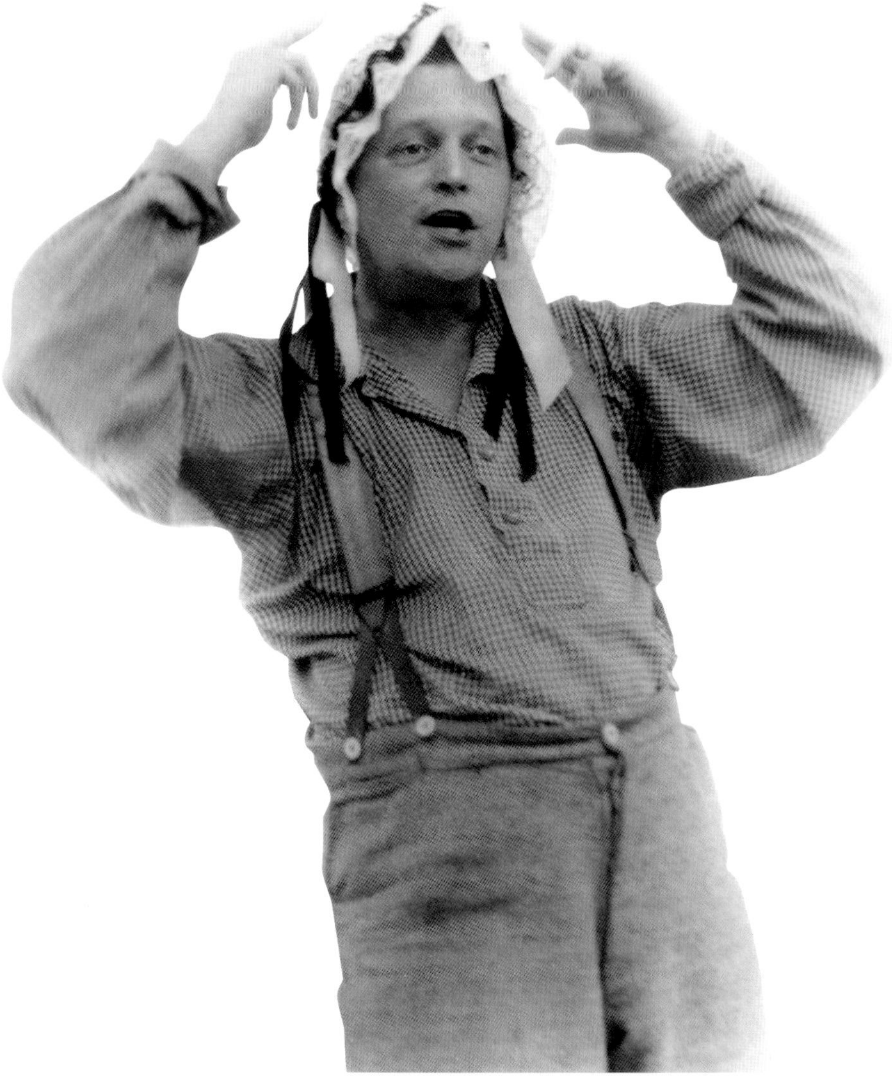

"**Z**ou! Zou! Zou!"

War cry of the Zouave troops

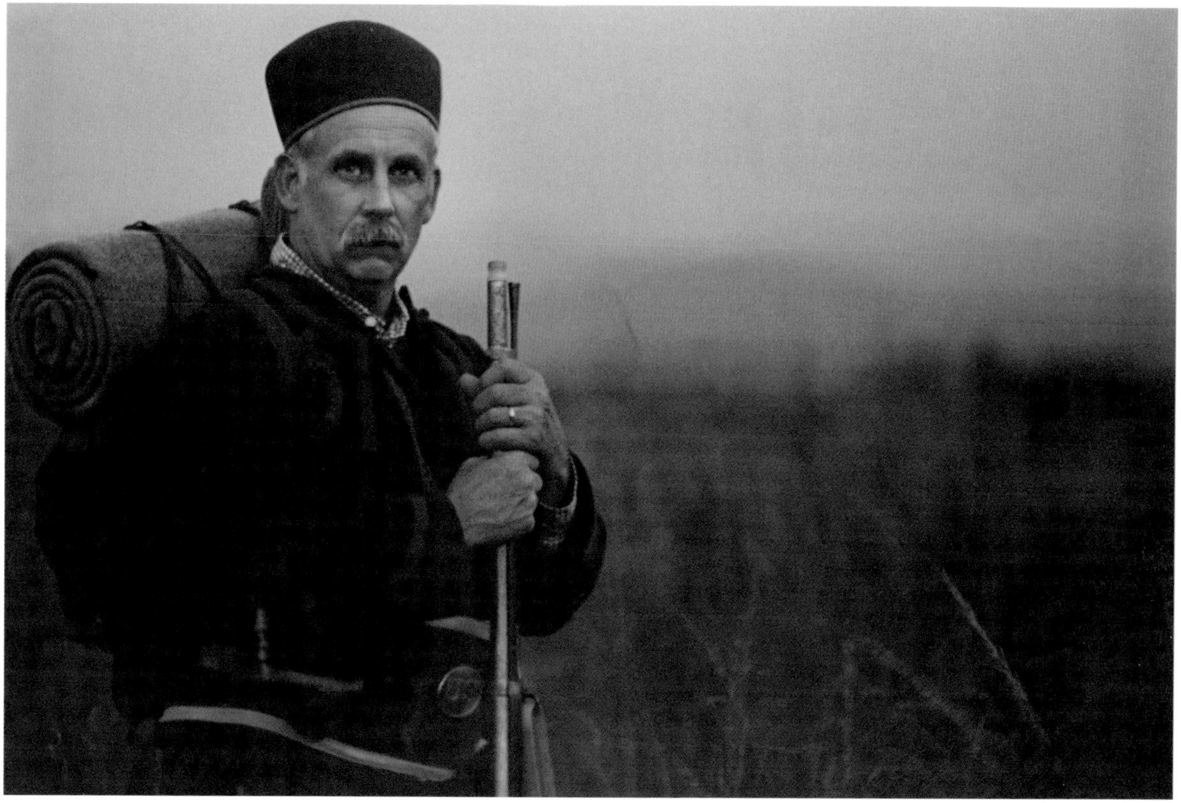

"Both before and after a battle, sad and solemn thoughts come to the soldier. Before the conflict they are of apprehension; after the strife there is a sense of relief; but the thinned ranks, the knowledge that the comrade who stood by your side in the morning never will stand here again, bring inexpressible sadness."

Charles Carleton Coffin
Army Correspondent

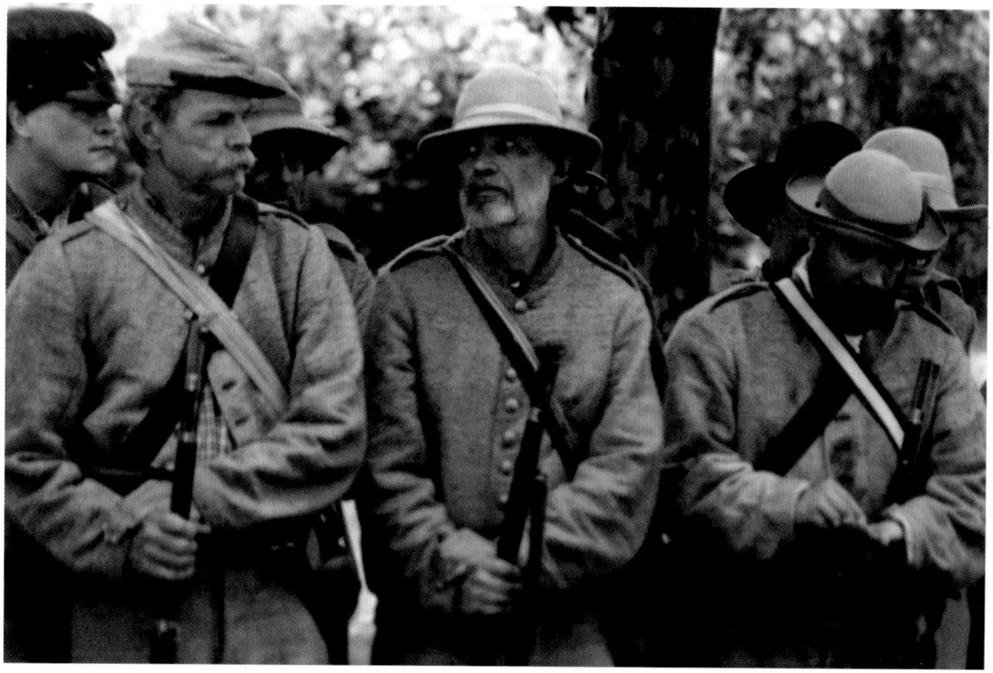

"The first thing in the morning
is drill then drill, then drill again.
Then drill, drill, a little more drill.
Then drill, and lastly drill."

    Pvt. Oliver Norton
    83rd Pennsylvania

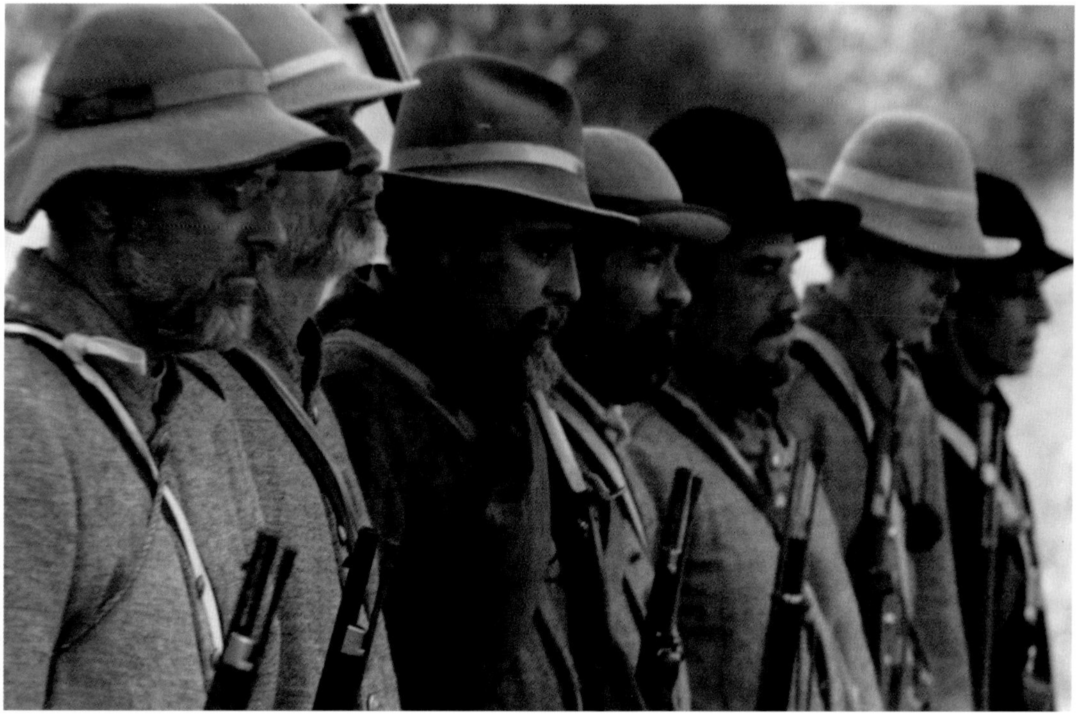

"One drill was hardly over before another was called. It was arduous labor, harder than grubbing, stump-pulling, or cracking rocks on a turnpike."

Private Alexander Hunter
17th Virginia Infantry Regiment

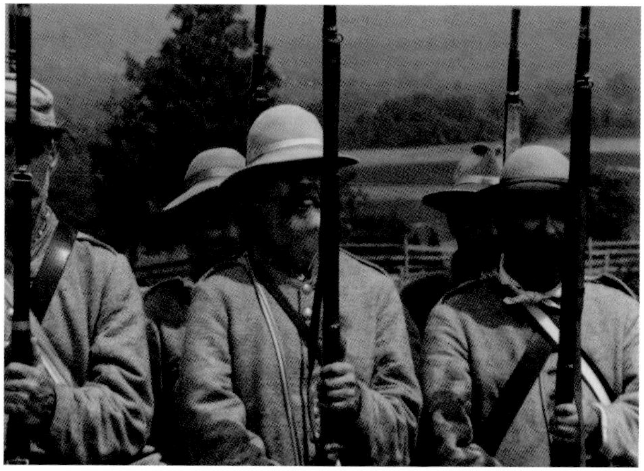

"We had barely loaded and capped the muskets when the blue line came with a rush and we fired now without orders."

Private Alexander Hunter
17th Virginia Infantry
Kemper's Brigade

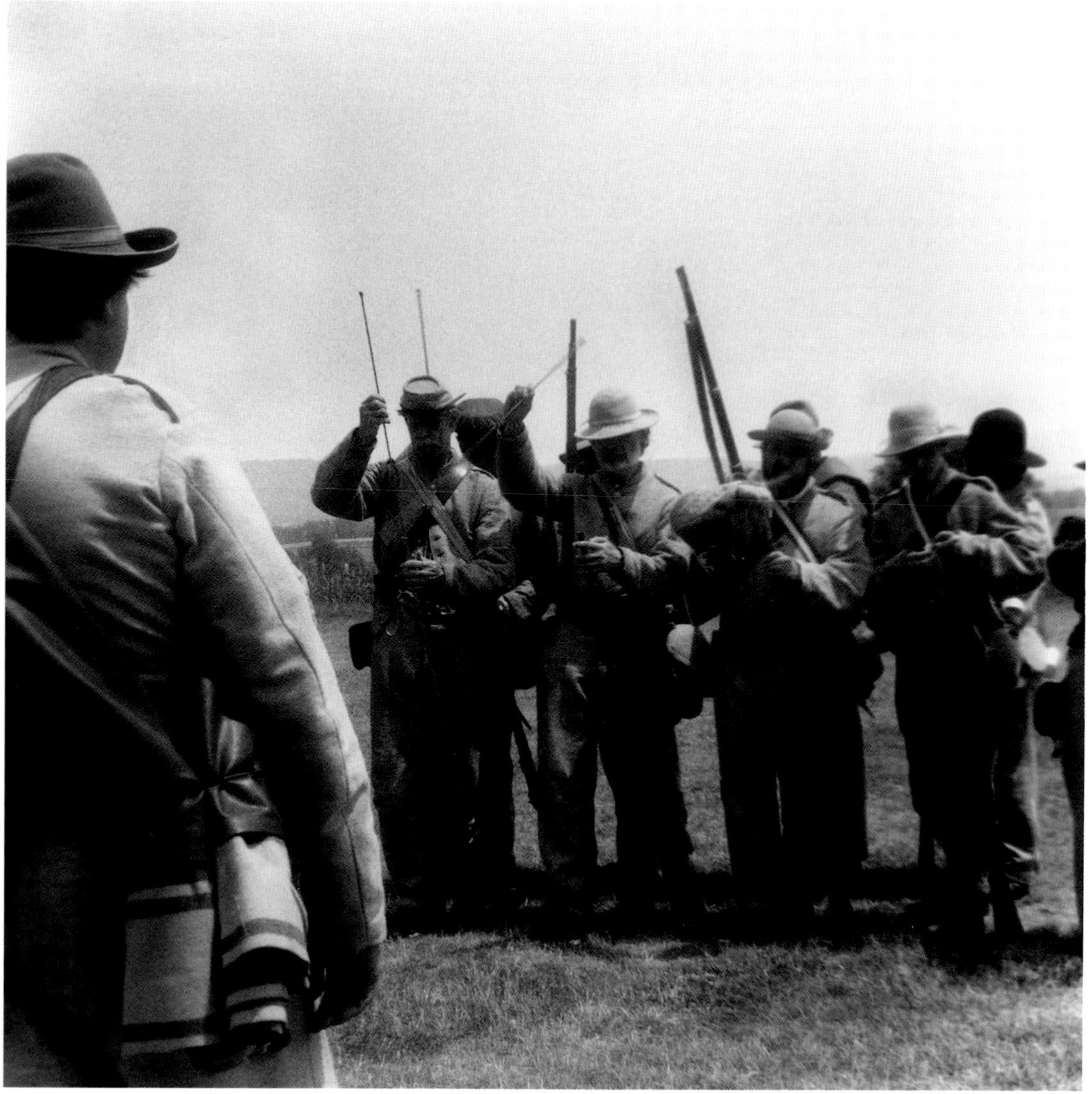

"Suddenly a stir beginning far up on the right, and running like a wave along the line, brought the regiment to its feet. A silence fell on everyone at once, for each felt that the momentous 'now' had come."

Private David L. Thompson
Company G
9th New York Volunteers

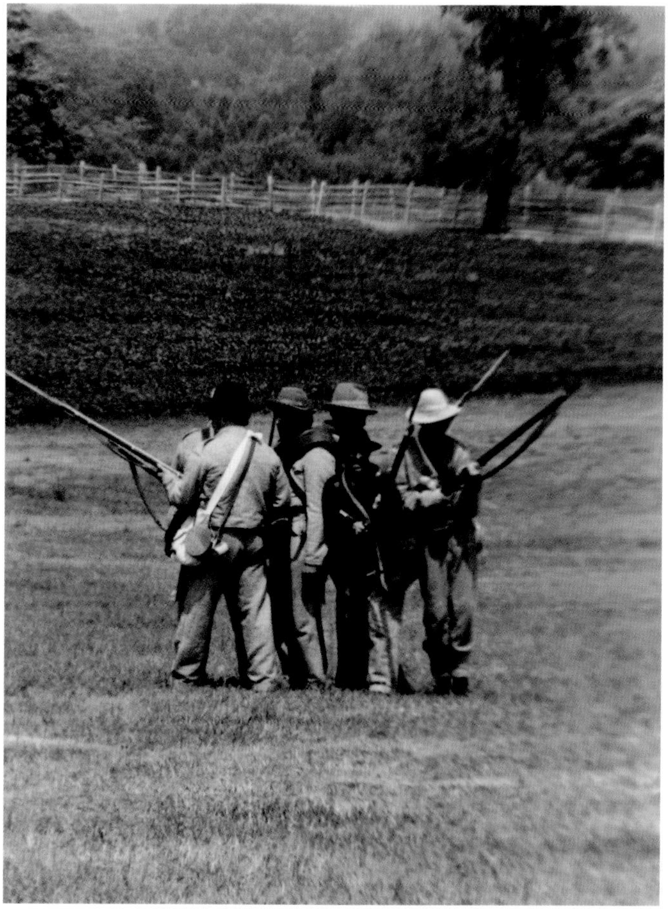

"I could see dimly through the dense sulphurous battle smoke and the line from Shakespear's *Tempest* flitted across my brain: 'Hell is empty and all the devils are here.'"

Private Frederick C. Foard
20th North Carolina Infantry
Galland's Brigade

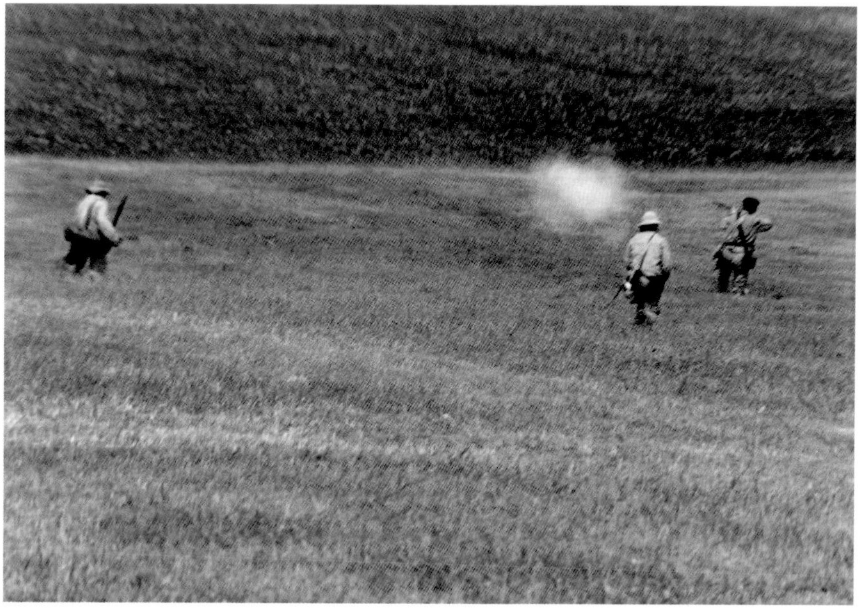

"None can realize the horrors of war, save those actually engaged. The dead lying all around, your foes unburied to the last, horses and wagons and troops passing heedlessly along. The stiffened bodies lie, grasping in death, the arms they bravely bore, with glazed eyes, and features blackened by rapid decay. Here sits one against a tree in motionless stare. Another has his head leaning against a stump, his hands over his head. They have paid the penalty. They have fought their last battle, The air is putrid with decaying bodies of men and horse. My God, My God, what a scourge is war."

A soldier
6th Georgia Infantry Regiment

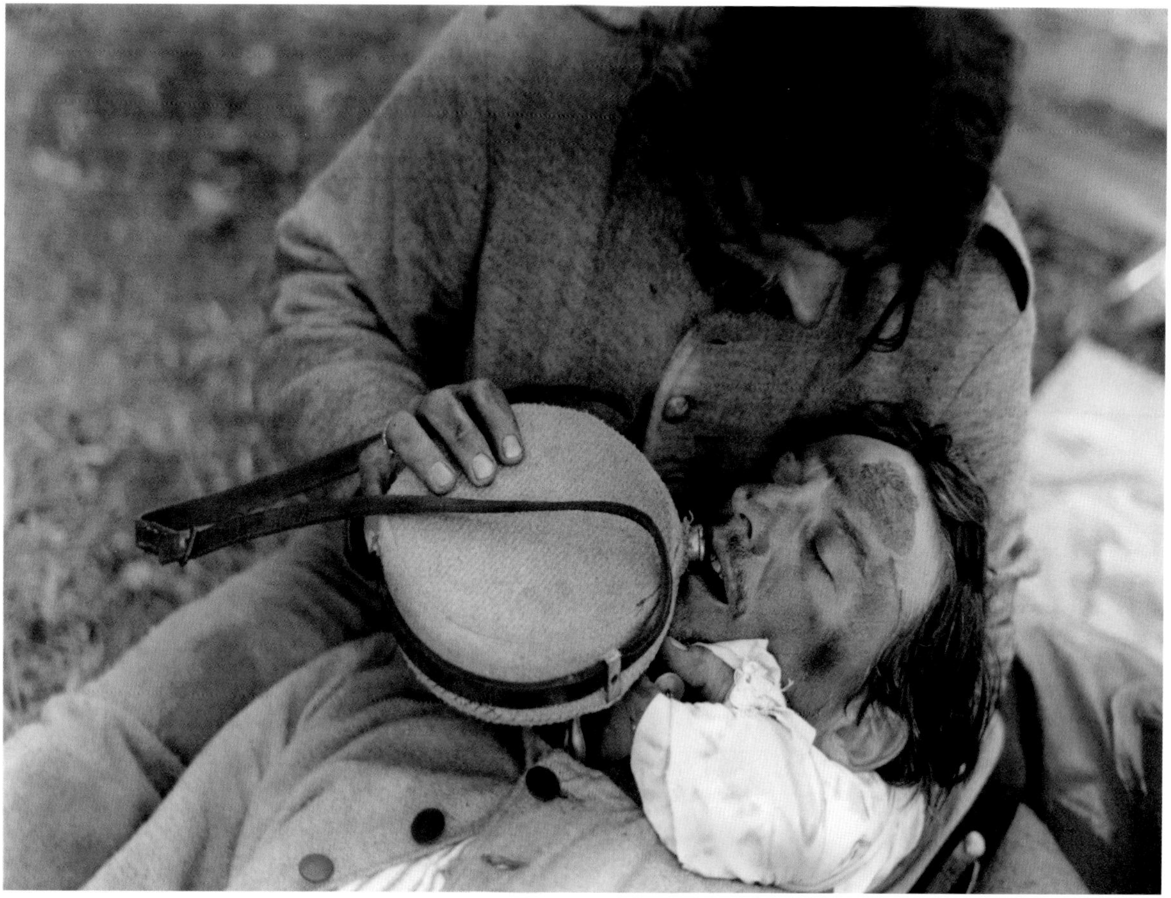

"The muster rolls on which the name and oath were written were pledges of honor – redeemable at the gates of death. And they who went up to them, knowing this, are on the lists of heroes."

Brigadier General Joshua Lawrence Chamberlain USA

COL. WALTER PHELPS JR.
COL. T. B. W. STOCKTON
COL. JOSEPH J. BARTLETT
COL. H. S. FAIRCHILD

"In the midst of the battle, a Confederate tried to climb over the fence at the further side of Bloody Lane, but was shot in the rear as he reached the top, his body hanging on the upper rail. When our regiment buried him, it was found that he had been riddled with seventeen bullets...This Lane was literally packed with their dead. At one point thirteen dead bodies lay on a heap, at other places they lay two, three, even five deep. No battle of the late war, of so short duration, presented such a scene of carnage."

Private Edward W. Spangler
Company K
130th Pennsylvania

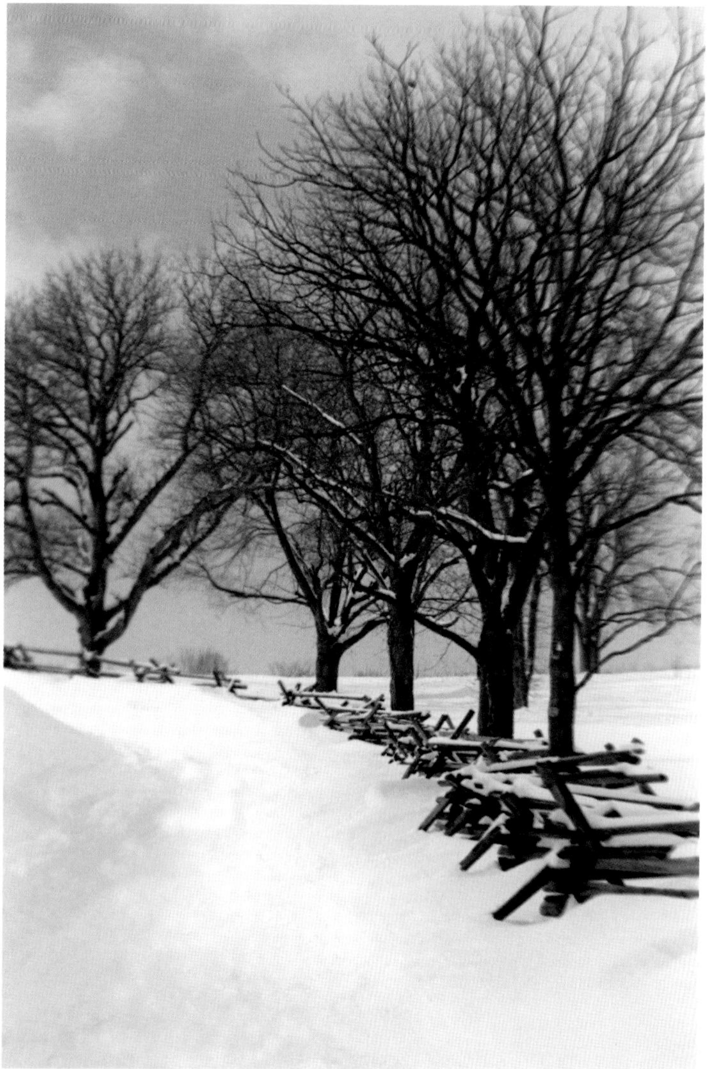

"When Johnny comes marching home again,
hurrah! hurrah!
We'll give him a hearty welcome then,
hurrah! hurrah!
The men will cheer, the boys will shout,
The ladies they will all turn out,
And we'll all feel gay when
Johnny comes marching home."

When Johnny Comes Marching Home
Patrick Sarsfield Gilmore
1863

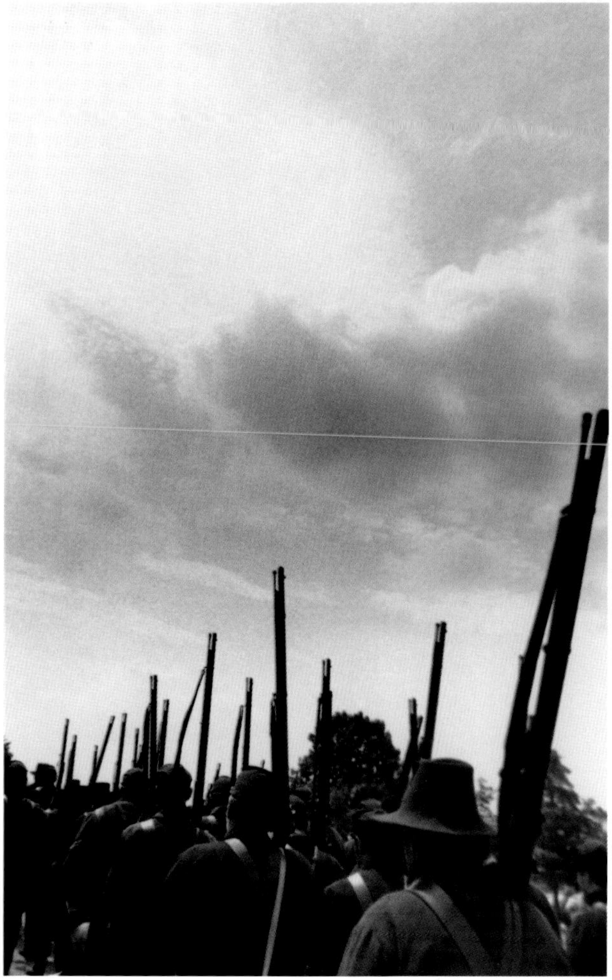

"Some of the men, with faces blackened by the powder from the tearing open of cartridges with the teeth in the act of loading their rifles, looked like demons rather than men, loading their guns and firing with a fearful, fiend-like intensity; some of the boys would load and fire with deliberation, while others, under an intense, insane excitement, would load and fire without aim."

Sergeant Major Elbridge Copp
3rd New Hampshire

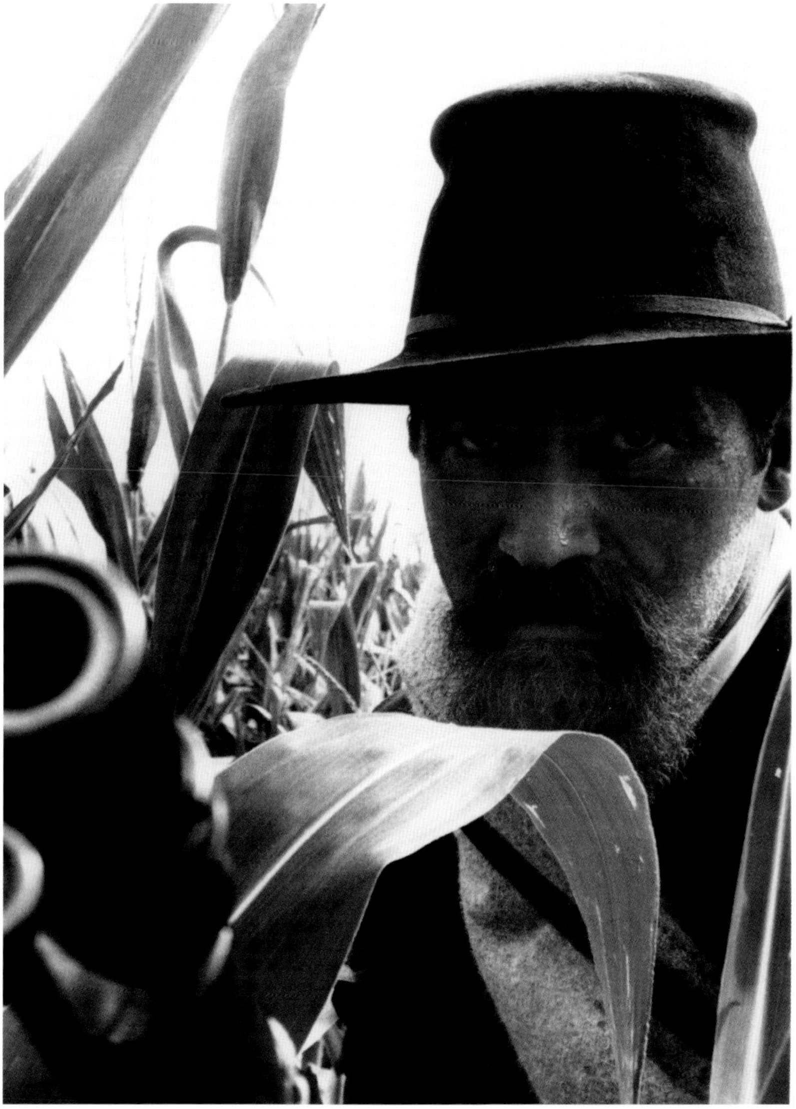

"A man lying upon the ground asked for a drink – I stooped to give it, and having raised him with my right hand, was holding the cup to his lips with my left, when I felt a sudden twitch of the loose sleeve of my dress – the poor fellow sprang from my hands and fell back quivering in the agonies of death – a ball had passed between my body – and the right arm which supported him – cutting through the sleeve, and passing through his chest from shoulder to shoulder."

Miss Clara Harlowe Barton
founder *The American Red Cross*
1821-1912

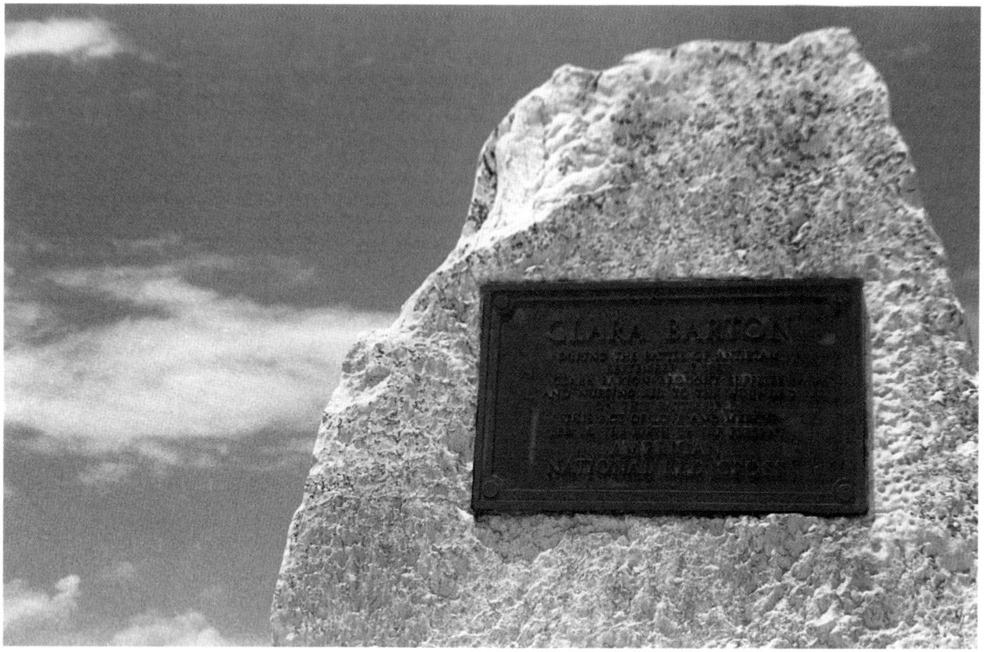
CLARA BARTON

"Those who lose friends in battle know what battlefields are...Mr. Brady has done something to bring home to us the terrible reality and earnestness of war. If he had not brought bodies and laid them in our dooryards and along streets, he has done something very like it...Homes have been made desolate, and the light of life in thousands of hearts has been quenched forever. All of this desolation imagination must paint – broken hearts cannot be photographed."

New York Times, October 20, 1862
From an article written in a review of an exhibit following a visit to Matthew Brady's New York Gallery, two months following the battle of Antietam

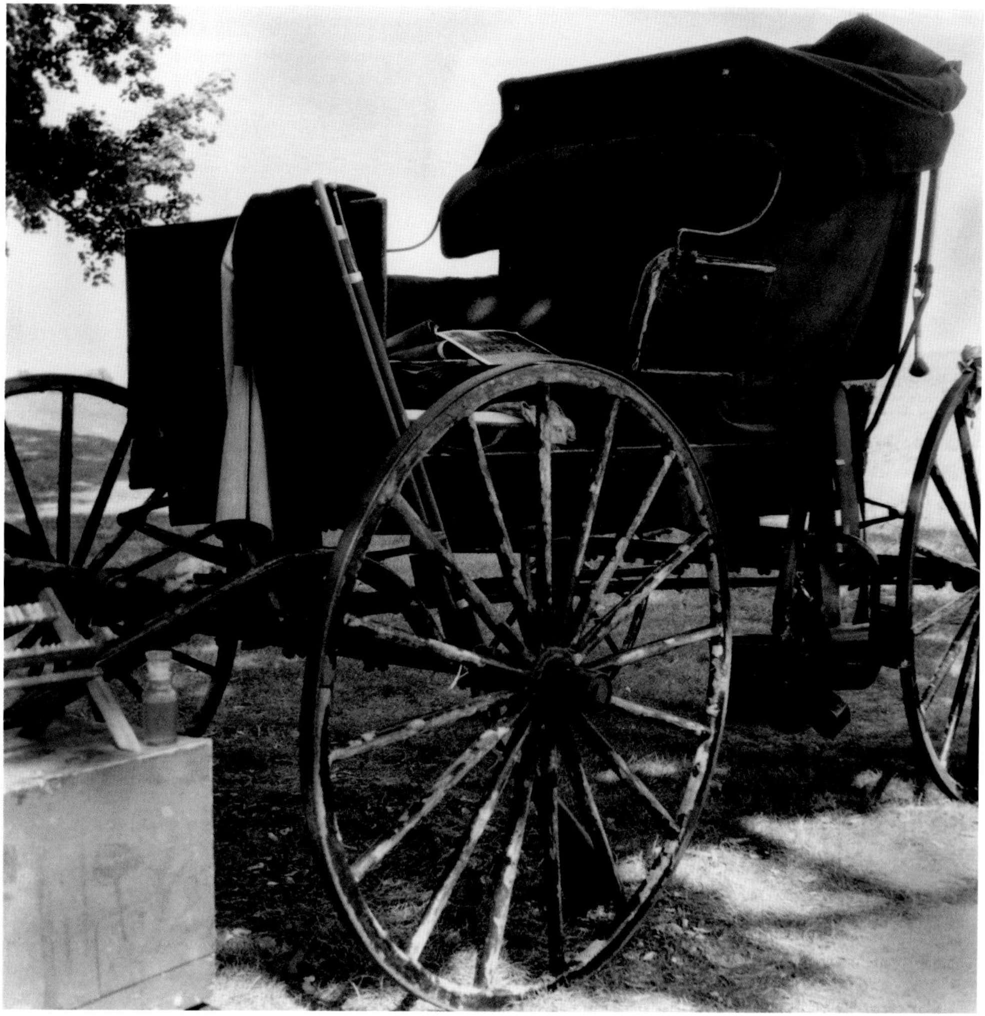

"There was, on the part of the men, great hysterical excitement, eagerness to go forward, and a reckless disregard of life, of every thing but victory."

Major Rufus R. Dawes
6th Wisconsin Infantry
Gibbon's Brigade

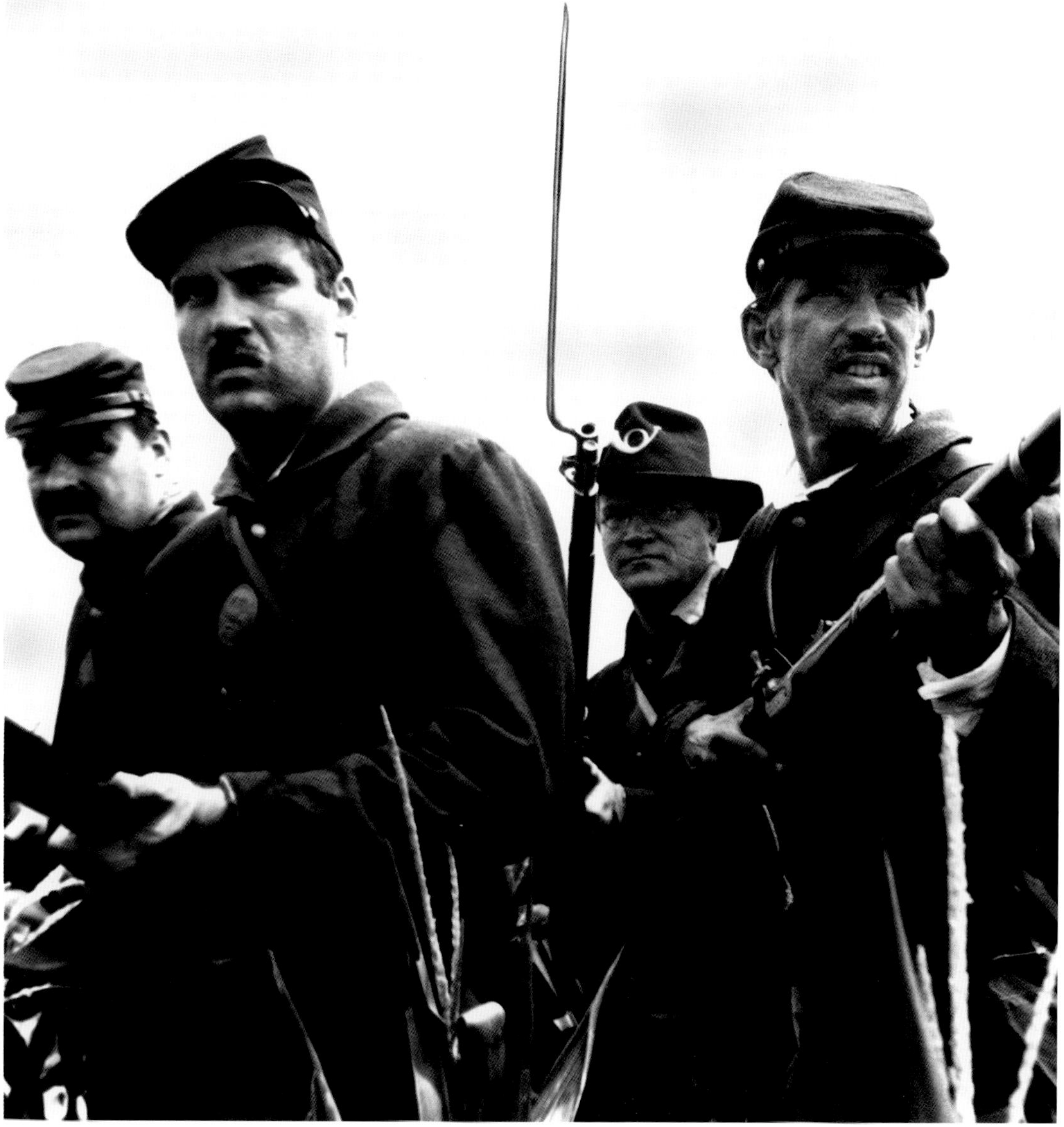

"They stayed until the rick was all eaten up."

Philip Pry
from his testimony to the
War Damage Claims Department

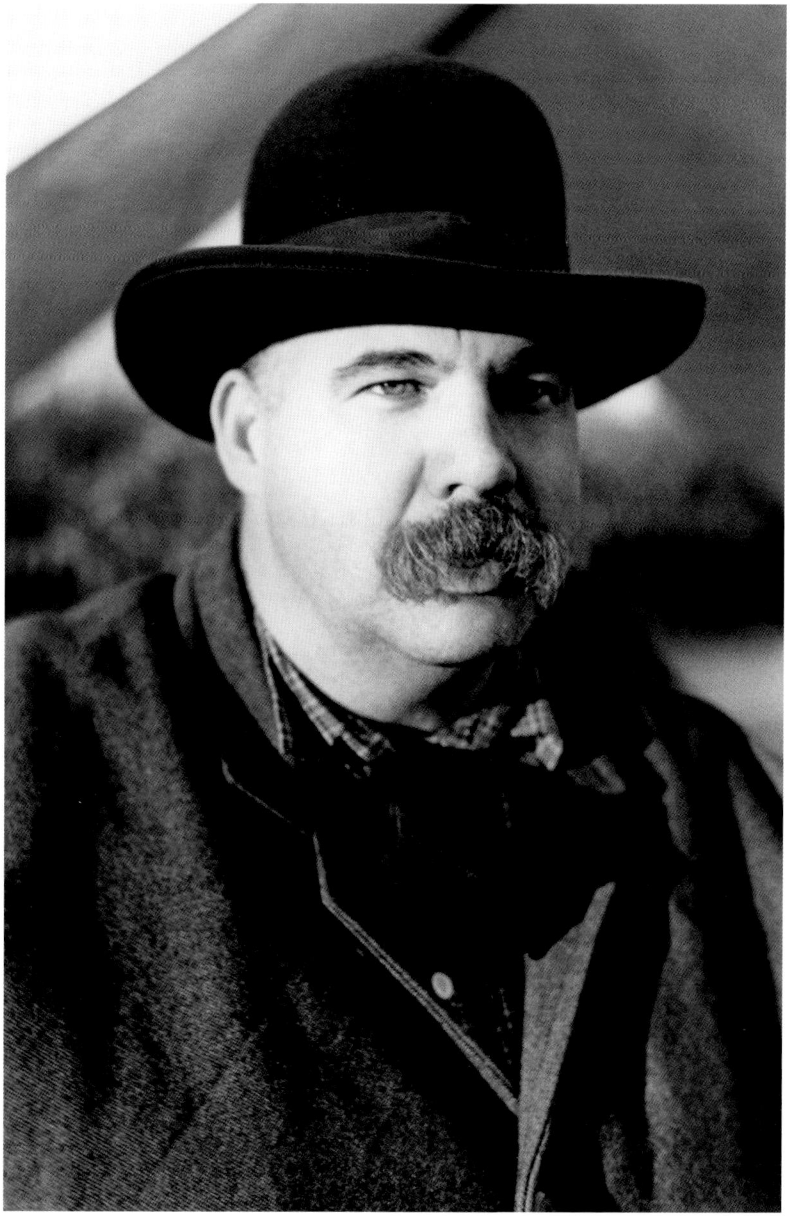

"It was near this spot that the regiment within 6 weeks after leaving home took an active part in this great battle."

124th Pennsylvania Volunteer Infantry
Casualties at Antietam
Killed 5
Wounded 42
Missing 17
Total 64

the monument in shadow

Commands

"The air was filled with a medley of sounds, shouts, cheers, commands, oaths, the sharp reports of rifles, the hissing shot, groans and prayers."

a Private from the 20th Maine

the move forward

"Under the shade of a towering oak near the Dunker Church lay the lifeless form of a drummer boy, apparently not more than 17 years of age, flaxen hair and eys of blue and form of delicate mould. As I approached him I stooped down and as I did so I perceived a bloody mark upon his forehead...it showed where the leaden messenger of death had produced the wound that caused his death. His lips were compressed, his eyes half open, a bright smile played upon his countenance. By his side lay his tenor drum, never to be tapped again."

Pvt. J. D. Hicks
Company K
125th Pennsylvania

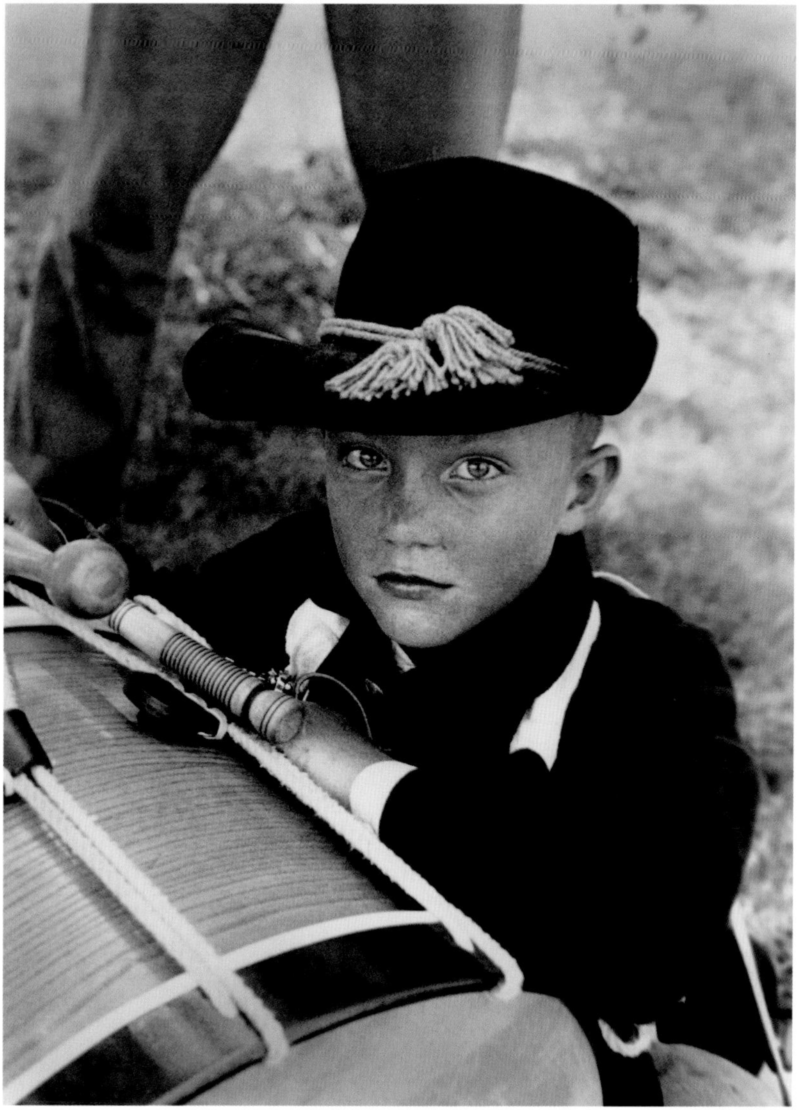

"A kind of desperation seized me. I snatched a gun form the hands of a man who was shot through the head. Then I jumped over dead men with as little feeling as I would over a log. The feeling that was uppermost in my mind was a desire to kill as many rebels as I could. The loss of comrades maddened me."

Private Oliver Norton
83rd Pennsylvania at Gaine's Mill
1862

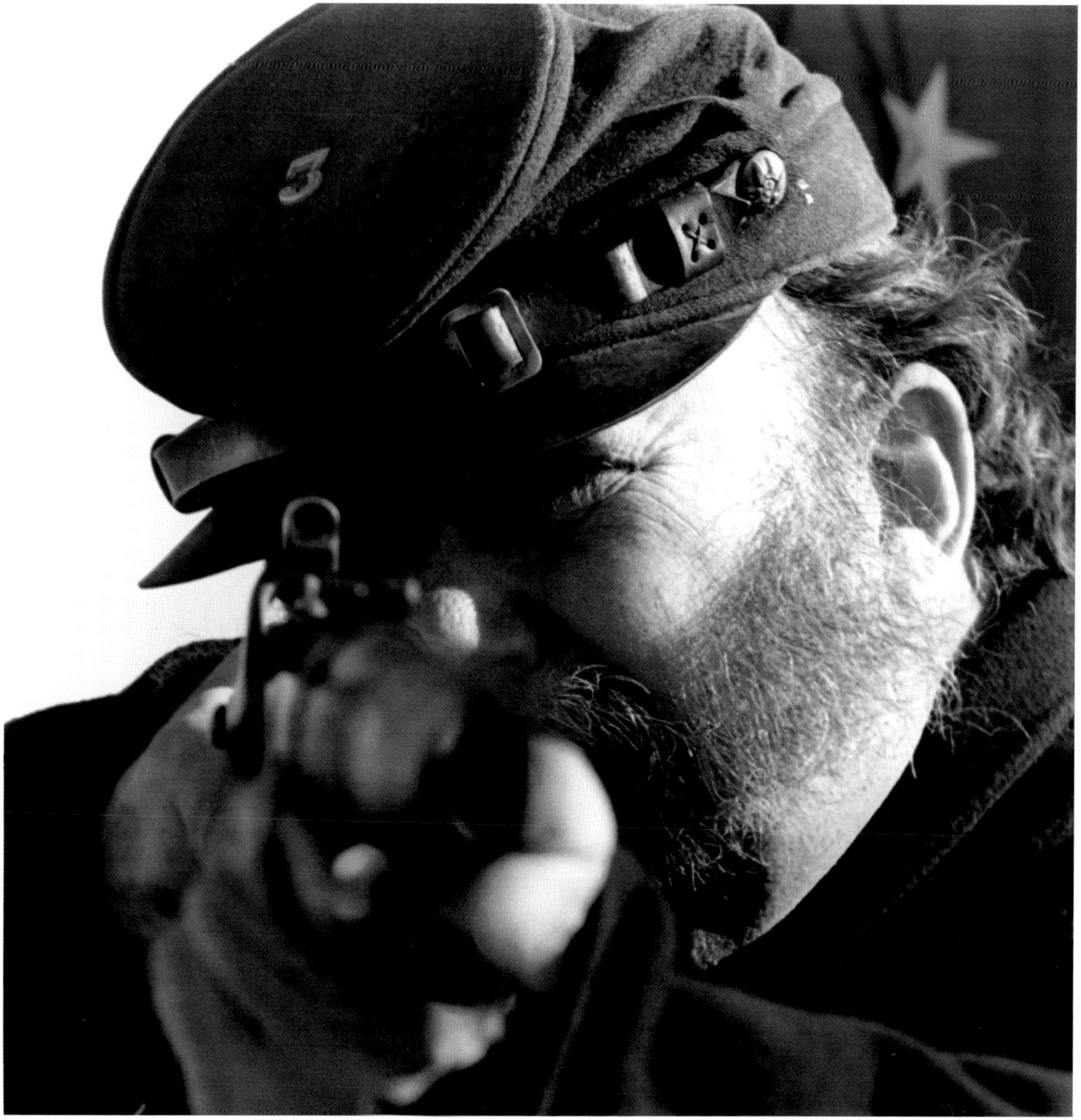

"...I want to say a word more about 'The Great Victory of Antietam' your nephew's idea of it. Both parties fought with a desperation. Both parties wavered at times. Each party chased the other, and were chased in turn. Each side slew the other by Thousands. After finaly each party lay down on the ground that the other had held (at different points of course, now both sides claim a monstrous Victory. Question. What was victorious? Answer. Neither."

R. E. Bowen
15th Massachusetts Volunteers
dated Boliver Heights, Oct. 8th
referring to Wednesday, September 17, 1862

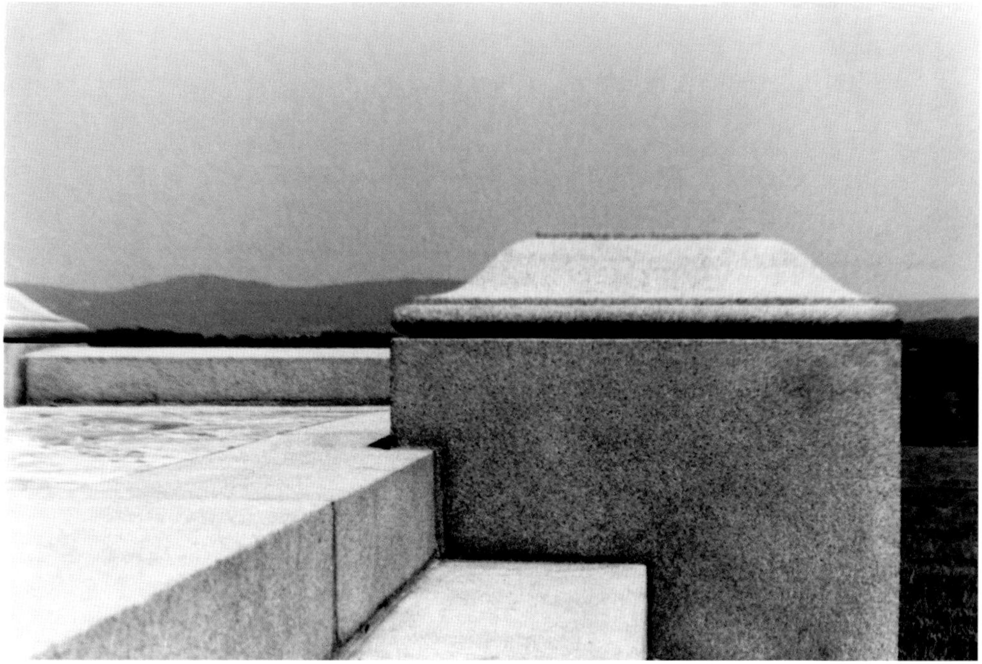

"All quiet on the Potomac."

1861,
Common saying early in the war, ridiculing McClellan's policy of delay; probably generated by McClellan's telegrams starting that "All is quiet tonight." Later the source of poet Ethel Lynn Beers *The Picket Guard*.

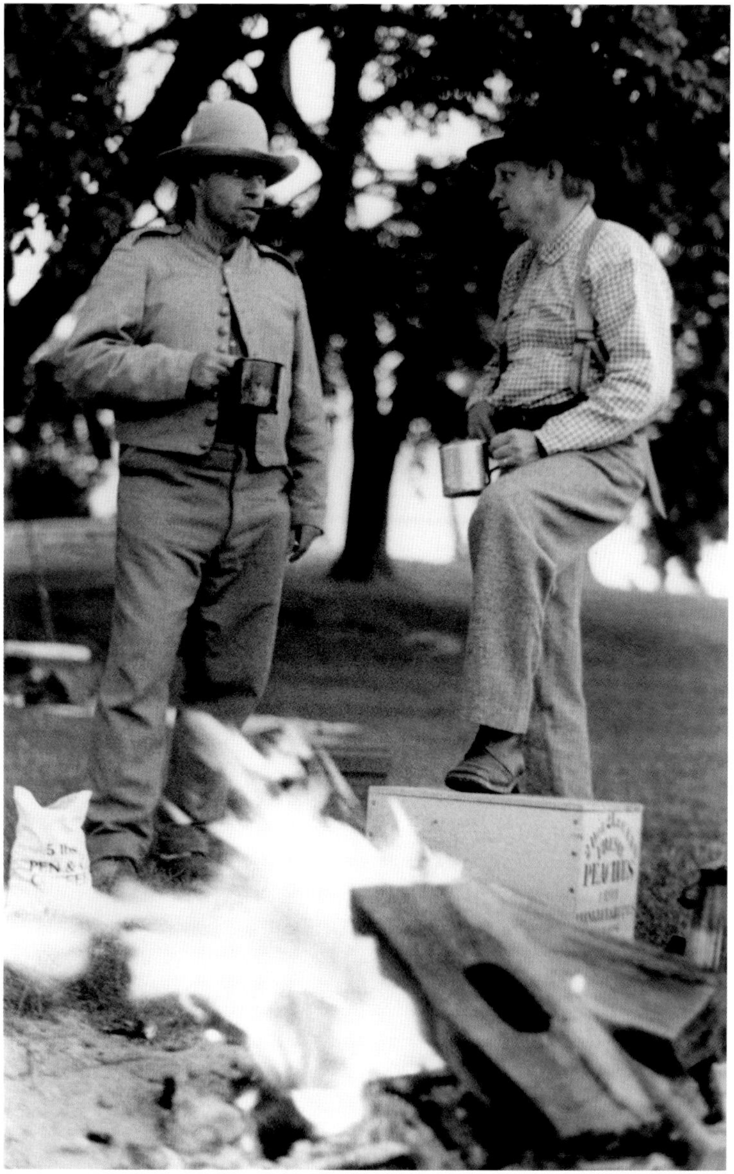
5 lbs
PEACHES

"When the soldiers are seeking rest, the work of the army correspondent begins. All through the day eyes and ear have been open. The notebook is scrawled with characters intelligible to him if read at once, but wholly meaningless a few hours later. He must grope his way along the lines in the darkness, visit the hospitals, hear the narratives of all, eliminate error, get at the probable truth, keeping ever in mind that each general thinks his brigade, each colonel his regiment, every captain his company, did most of the fighting."

Charles Carleton Coffin
Army Correspondent

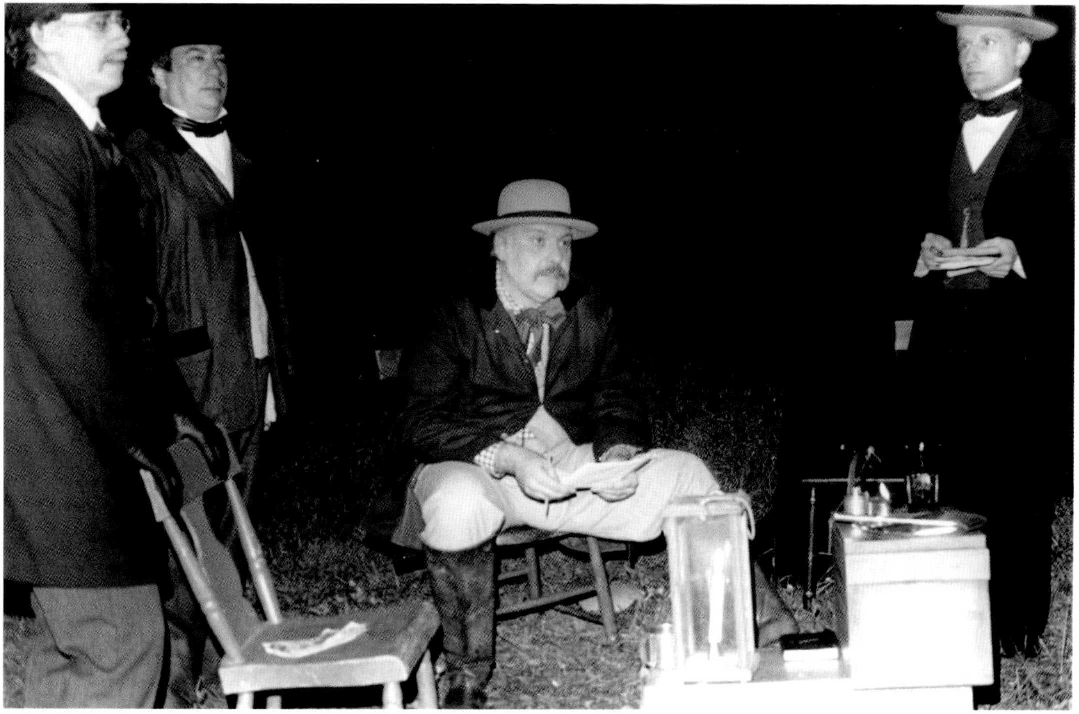

"I have called on you for some help I am a widir woman with sixth children I was doin pirty well but since this war bisness commence it has cost me a good bit of truble I am willing to do with less for the sake of are union to stand I want you please to help me a little as I standly badly in need of som help."

Mrs. Sarah H. Vandergrift
a civilian, Chester, Pennsylvania
8 July 1861
a letter to President Lincoln

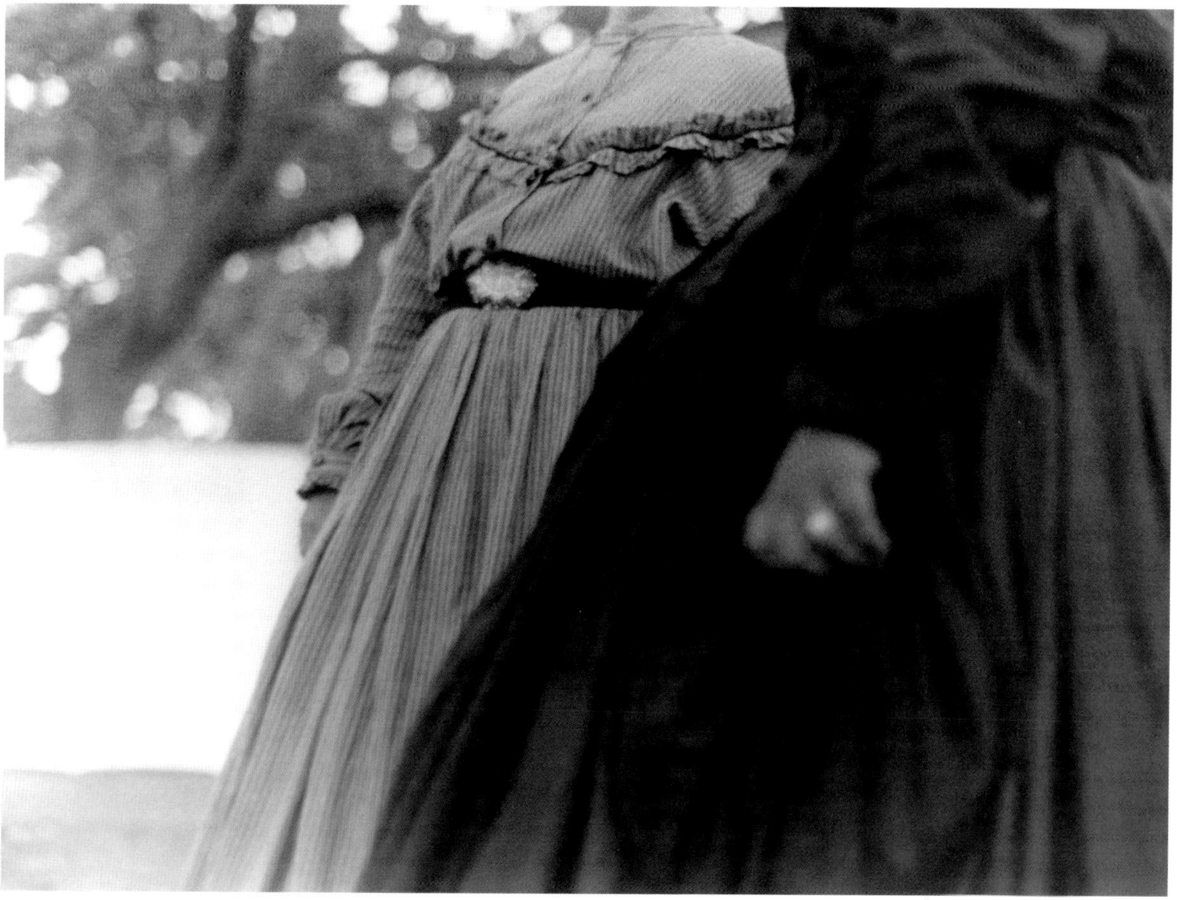

"Behind all these men you have to do with, behind officers, and government, and people even, there is the country herself, your country, and you belong to her as you belong to your own mother. Stand by her boy, as you would stand by your mother."

Edward Everett Hale
The Man Without A Country
1863

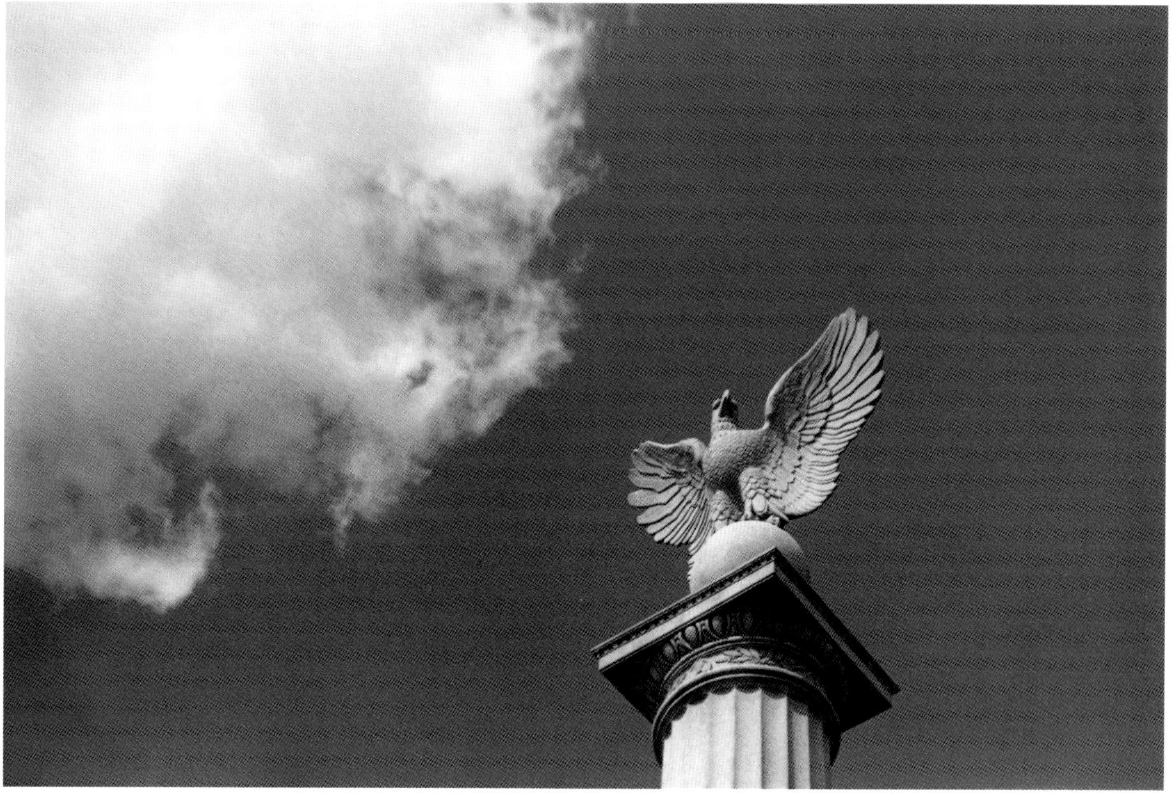

"Perhaps you don't know how we bury the dead. Let me tell you about this particular *trench* and that ill suffice for the whole. The trench in which Henry is buried is situated near a log cabin just out side of the garden fence. I believe its on the West side. The trench was 25 feet long, 6 feet wide and about 3 feet deep. The corpes [corpses] were buried by Co... they are laid in two tiers, one [on] top of the other...Henry is 3rd corpes from the upper end on the top tier next to the woods...there is a board put up at each end of the trench with the simple inscription, '15th mass. Buried here.'...Some of the men had their clothes taken off by the rebels. Henry did not have anything taken but shoes and what was in his pockets."

R. E. Bowen
Bolivar Heights, VA
Sept. 28, 1862
A letter to Henry Ainsworth's father

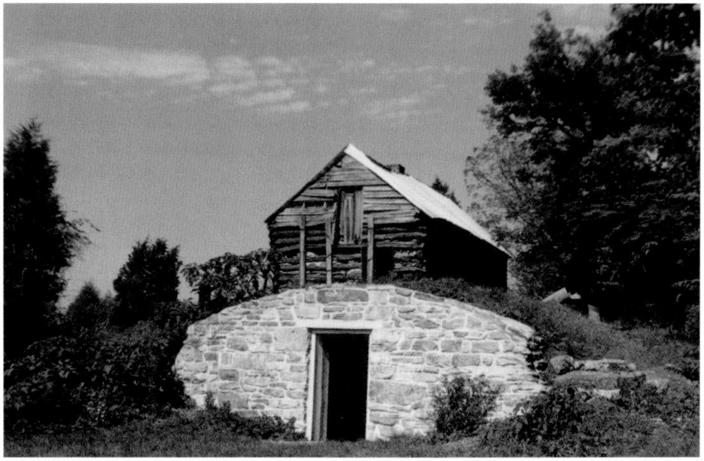

"Here September 17, 1862, the Fifteenth Regiment Massachusetts Volunteers, with the first Company Andrew Sharpshooters, attacked 606 men of all ranks, commanded by Lt. John W. Kimball, Gorman's Brigade, Sedgewick's Division, Second Army Corps, met and engaged troops of the Brigades of Semmes, Early and Barksdale. Within 20 minutes 330 had fallen, 75 killed and 255 wounded, 43 dying of wounds."

The Monument to the 15th Massachusetts Volunteers

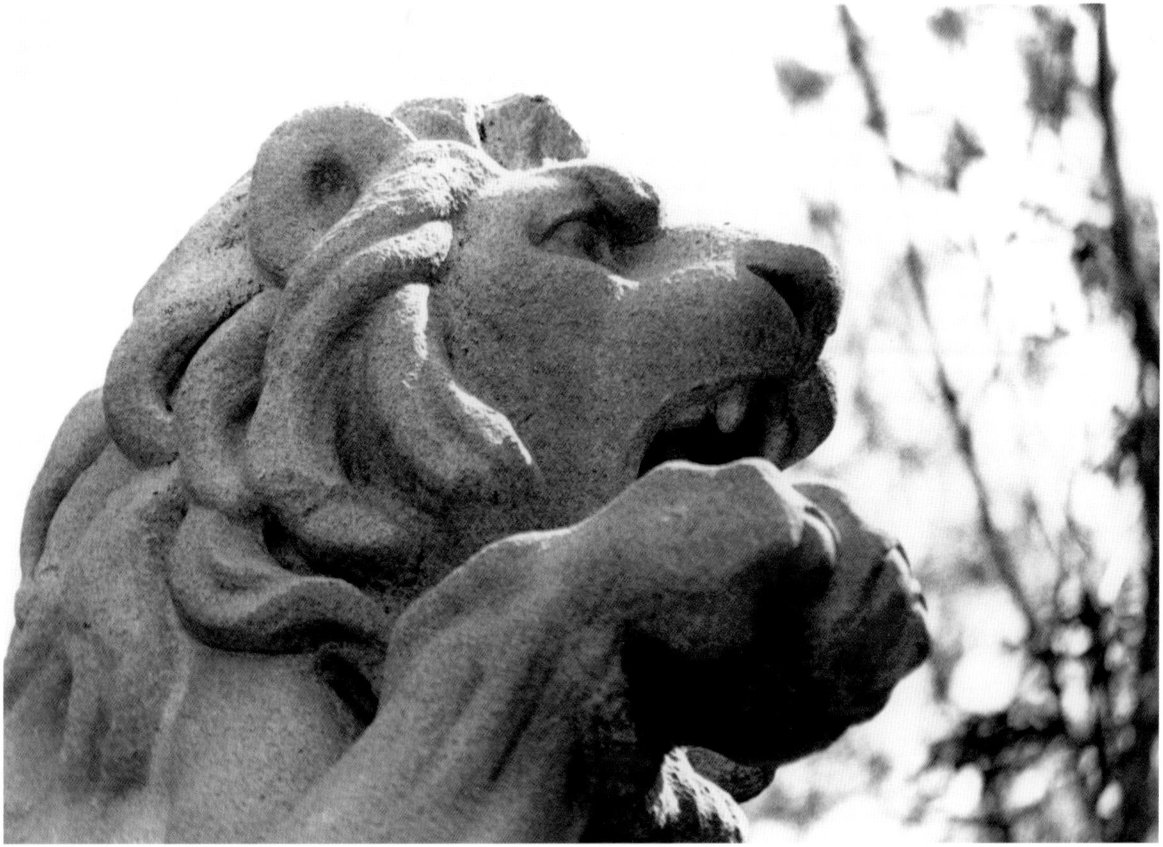

"The rebellion which has convulsed the nation for four years, threatened the Union, and caused such sacrifice of blood and treasure may be traced in a great degree to the diseased imagination of certain South Carolina gentlemen, who some thirty and forty years since studied Scott's novels, and fancied them cavaliers imbued with chivalry, a superior class, not born to labor but to command, brave beyond mankind generally, more intellectual, more generous, more hospitable, more liberal than others."

Gordon Welles
journalist, politician, Secretary of the Navy, 1861-1869
April 1865, from his diary

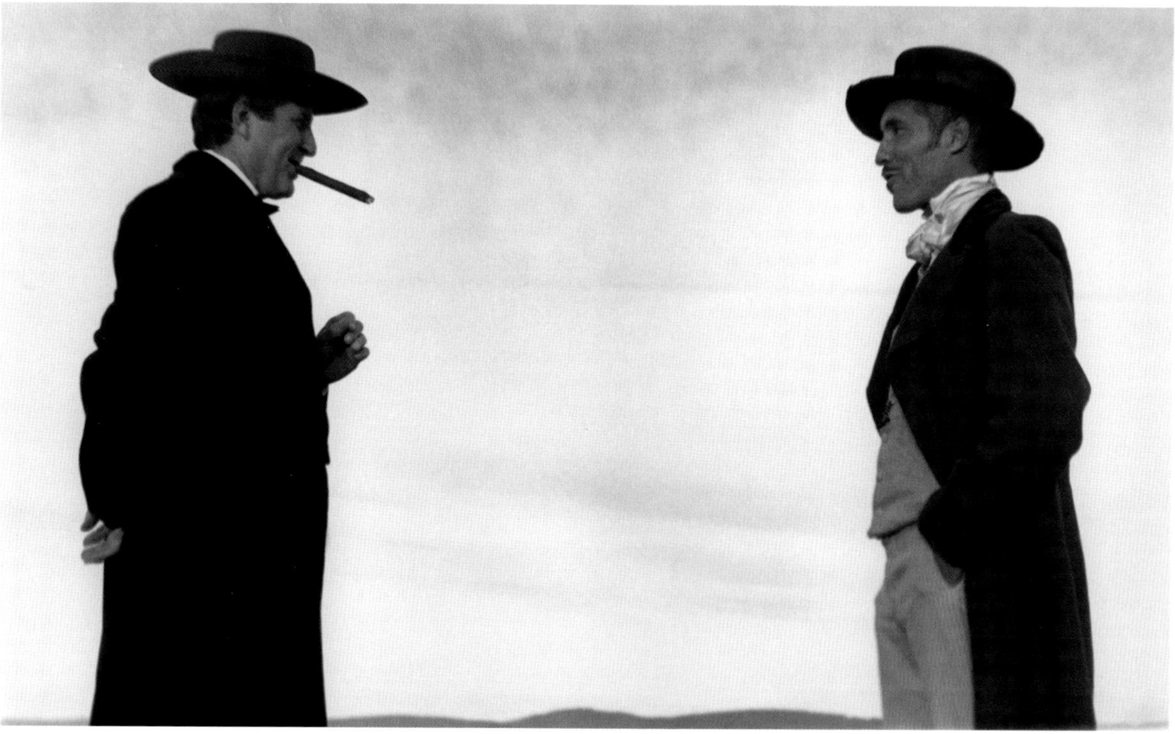

"If you take the bridge, you will accomplish one of the greatest feats of the war, and our name will be recorded in history. If the bridge is lost, all is lost."

Major General George Brinton McClellan

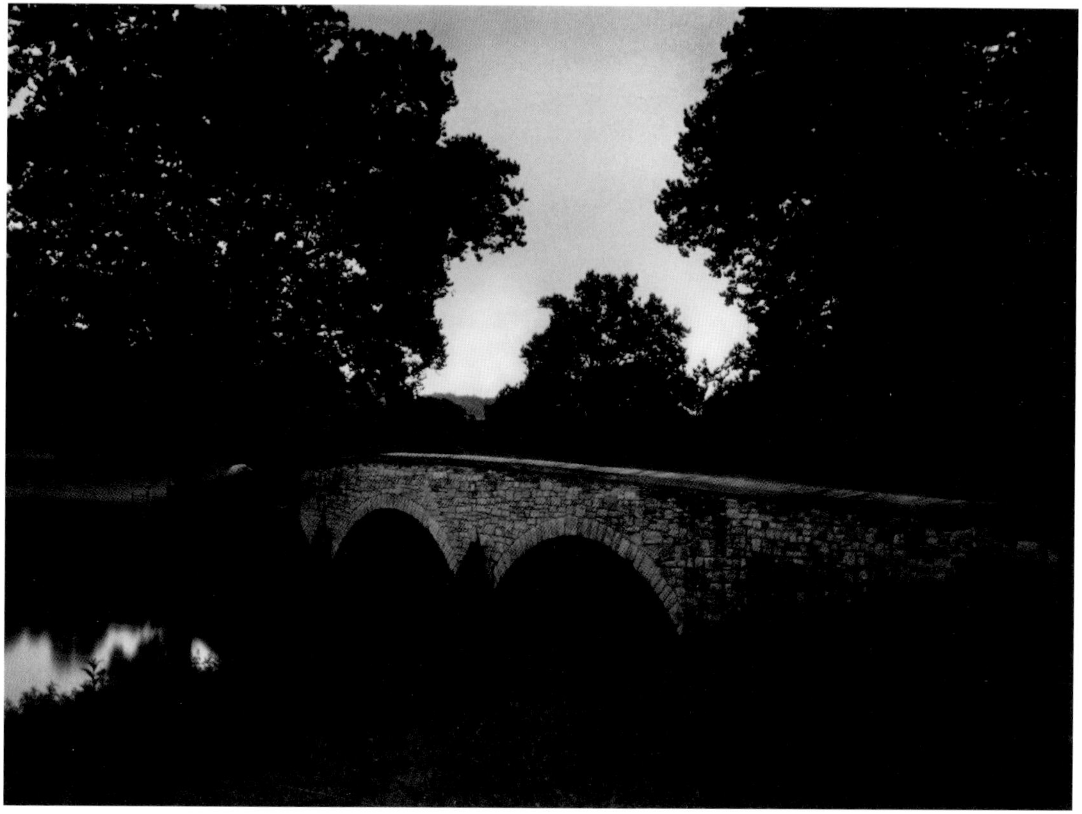

"He is one of the thousands of our unknown American young men in the ranks about whom there is no record of fame, no fuss made about their dying so unknown, but I find in them the real precious & royal ones of this land, giving themselves up, aye even their young & precious lives, in their country's cause."

Walt Whitman
10 August 1863
letter to the parents of Erastus Haskell

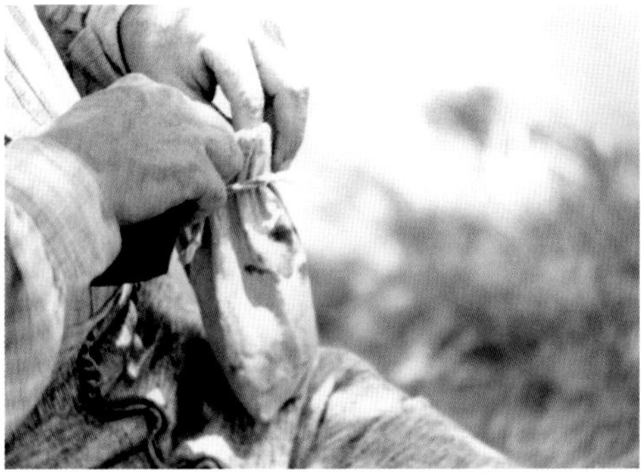

"I remember the battle of Antietam...the Union forces were encamped for several weeks after the battle...During this time all the cattle and sheep were taken and used by U.S. military forces...I remember four of the calves were slaughtered in the orchard back of the blacksmith shop."

Mary Ellen Piper Smith
daughter of Henry Piper
21 years old at time of the battle

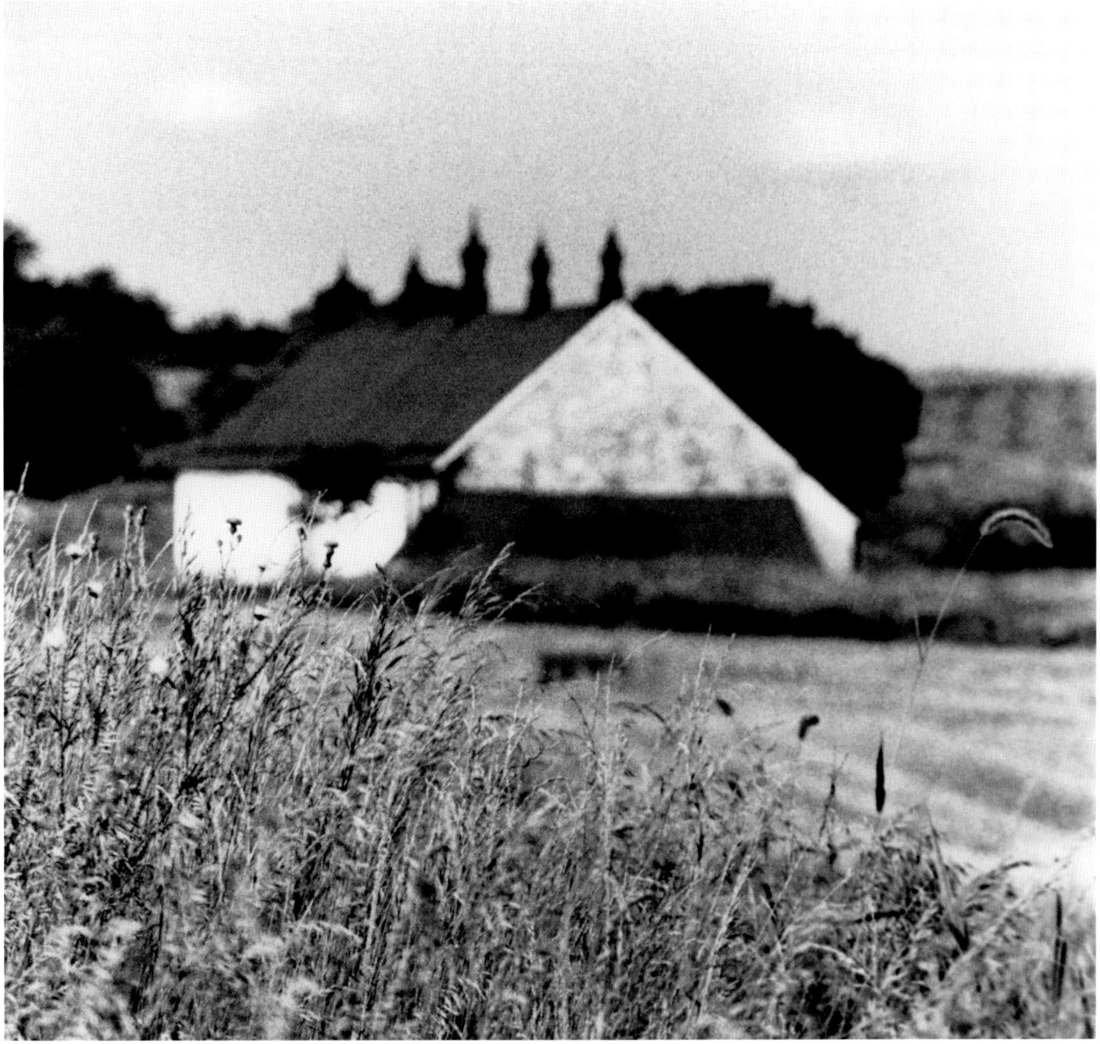

"In this sad world sorrow comes to all, but we have saved the Union."

President Abraham Lincoln

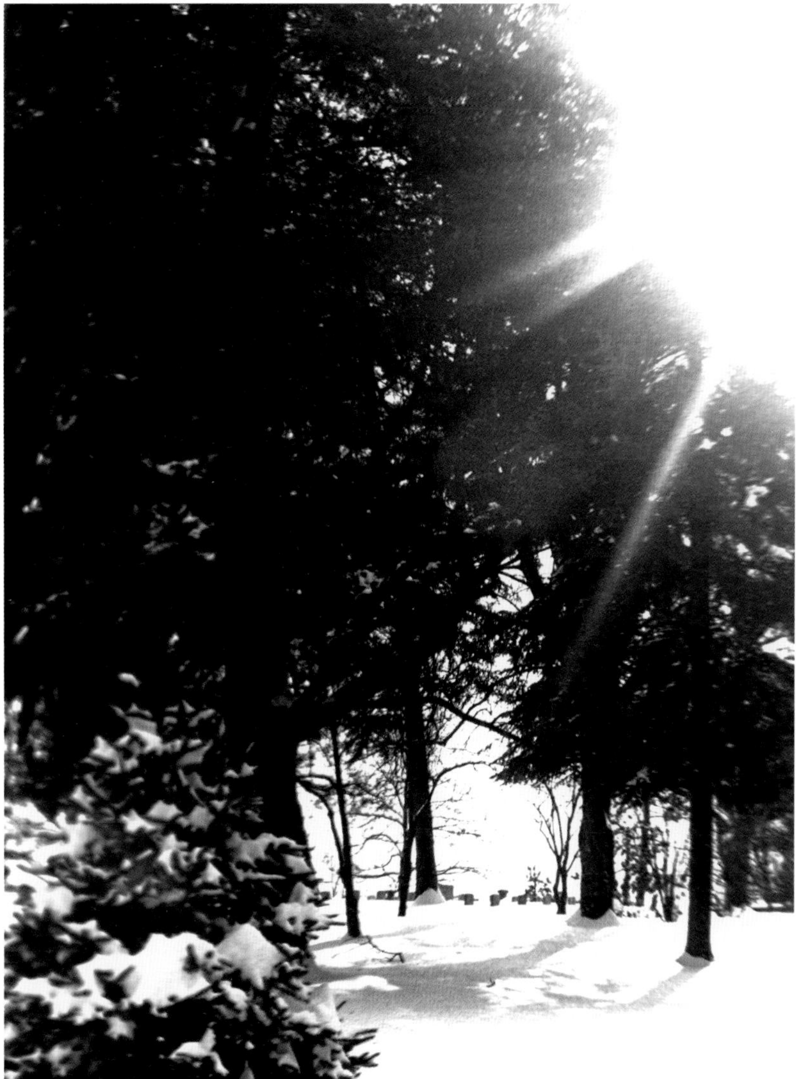

Grave of Freed Slave
Jeremiah Cornelius Summers

Born July 22, 1847. Died November 8, 1925. Married October 25, 1870 to Susan Keets. Father of one daughter and one son. Taken by Union soldiers during the Maryland Campaign. Former owner, Henry Piper, traveled to Frederick to gain Summer's release. After the war, Mr. Summers made his living continuing to work on the Piper Farm and hiring himself out as a paid hand. When Piper died, he gave "Jerry" a lifelong home in a cottage on the Piper Farm along with a small garden plot. Mr. Summers is buried in the small graveyard behind Tolson's Chapel in Sharpsburg, Maryland, the building the last Freedmen's Bureau School standing in Maryland.

"I close. We are not, we must not be aliens or enemies but fellow countrymen and brethren. Although passion has strained our bonds of affection too hardly they must not, I am sure they must not be broken. The mystic chords which proceeding from so many battlefields and so many patriot graves pass through all the hearts and all the hearths in this broad continent of ours will yet again harmonize in their ancient music when breathed upon by the guardian angel of the nation."

February 1861
draft closing 1st inaugural address
President-elect Abraham Lincoln

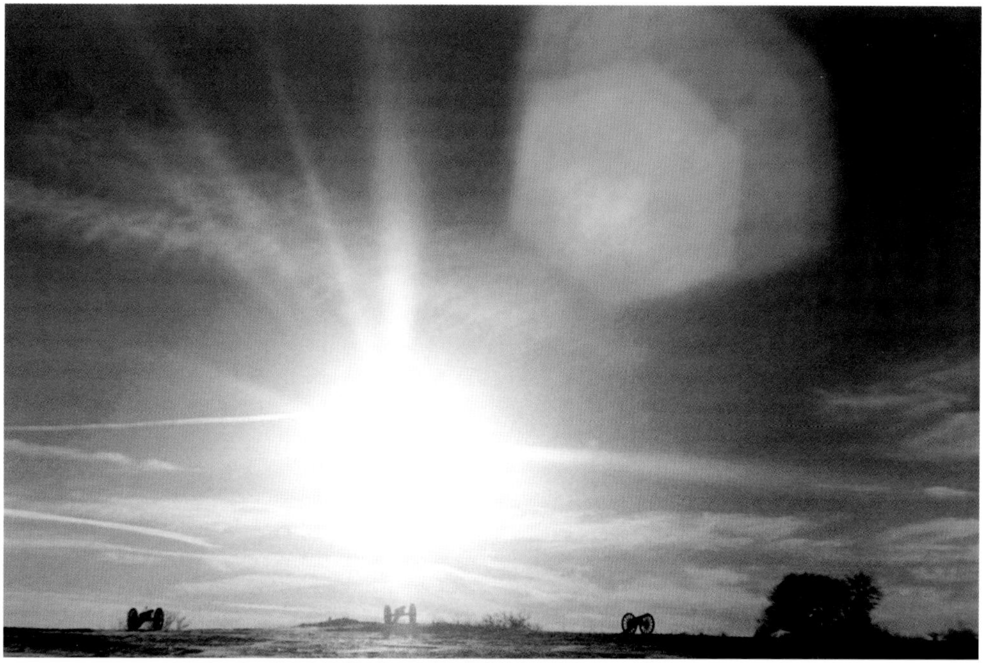

selected bibliography

American Heritage, *The American Heritage Picture History of the Civil War*, New York: American Heritage Publishing Co., Inc., 1960.

Bailey, Ronald H., and the Editors of Time-Life Books, *The Civil War, The Bloodiest Day, The Battle of Antietam*, Alexandria, VA: Time-Life Books, 1984.

Billings, John D., *Hard Tack and Coffee or The Unwritten Story of Army Life*, Williamstown, Mass: Corner House Publishers., 1984.

Blue & Gray Magazine's History and Tour Guide of the Antietam Battlefield, Columbus, Ohio., 1995.

Botkin, B. A., *A Civil War Treasury of Tales, Legends and Folklore*, New York: Random House, 1960.

Country Beautiful, *Civil War, The Years Asunder*, Waukesha, WI: Country Beautiful., 1973.

Country Beautiful, *Lincoln: His Words and His World*, Waukesha, WI: Country Beautiful., 1965.

Frassanito, William A., Antietam, *The Photographic Legacy of America's Bloodiest Day*, Gettysburg, PA.: Thomas Publications, 1978.

Harsh, Joseph L., *Taken at the Flood, Robert E. Lee and The Maryland Campaign of 1862*, Kent, Oh.: The Kent State University Press, 1999.

Lyman, Darryl, *Civil War Quotations*, Conshohocken, PA: Combined Books, inc., 1995.

Mitchell, Patricia., Confederate Home Cooking, Chatham, VA: Patricia B. Mitchell, 1991.

National Park Service, *Antietam As They Saw It*, United States Department of the Interior Publication.

Robertson Jr., James I and the Editors of Time-Life Books, *The Civil War, Tenting Tonight*, Alexandria, VA: Time-Life Books, 1984.

Stepp, John & Hill, I. William, *Mirror of War, The Washington Star Reports The Civil War*, Castle Books, Inc., 1961.

Time-Life Books, *Voices of the Civil War – Antietam*, Alexandria, VA: Time-Life Books., 1996.

Time-Life Books, *Echoes of Glory, Arms and Equipment of the Union*, Alexandria, VA: Time-Life Books, 1991.

Time-Life Books, *Echoes of Glory, Arms and Equipment of the Confederacy*, Alexandria, VA: Time-Life Books, 1991.

Ward, Geoffrey C with Ric and Ken Burns, *The Civil War: An Illustrated History*, New York: Alfred A. Knopf, Inc., 1990.

Wiley, Bell Irvin, *The Life of Johnny Reb*, Baton Rouge and London: Louisiana State University Press, 1978.

Author's Note: Some quotations were found in the Battlefield's archives and through information supplied by the staff of Antietam National Battlefield. All quotations have been reproduced as originally written.